Great Women Athletes of the 20th Century

Great Women Athletes of the 20th Century

by

Robert J. Condon

McFarland & Company, Inc., Publishers

Jefferson, North Carolina, and London

British Library Cataloguing-in-Publication data are available

Library of Congress Cataloguing-in-Publication Data

Condon, Robert J., 1934–
    Great women athletes of the 20th century / by Robert J. Condon.
      p. cm.
    Includes index.
    ISBN 0-89950-555-4 (lib. bdg. : 50# alk. paper) ∞
    1. Women athletes – Biography.   2. Women athletes – History – 20th
century. I. Title.
GV697.A1C68 1991
796.092′2 – dc20
[B]   91-52633
                                              CIP

Manufactured in the United States of America

McFarland & Company, Inc., Publishers
  Box 611, Jefferson, North Carolina 28640

To the women in my life:
Mae, Mary, Anne, Linda, Wendy,
Christine, Kathleen and Caroline

Contents

Preface ix

Introduction: Women in Sports 1

The Top Five

Mildred Ella Didrikson Zaharias 10

Dawn Fraser 13

Sonja Henie 15

Jacqueline Joyner-Kersee 19

Helen Wills Moody 22

The Pioneers

Glenna Collett Vare 28

Charlotte Dod 32

Amelia Mary Earhart 34

Gertrude Ederle 37

Eleanor Holm 40

Suzanne Rachel Flore Lenglen 43

Annie Oakley 47

Eleonora Randolph Sears 50

Helen Herring Stephens 54

Joyce Wethered 58

Thirty-five More Great Women Athletes

Tenley Emma Albright 62

Joan Benoit Samuelson 65

Fanny Blankers-Koen 69

Florence Mary Chadwick 71

Nadia Comanecei 74

Maureen Connolly 78

Margaret Smith Court 81

Mary Teresa Decker 85

Kornelia Ender 88

Christine Marie Evert 91

Peggy Gale Fleming 94

Althea Gibson 97

Steffi Graf 100

Delorez Florence Griffith-Joyner
104
Dorothy Hamill   107
Carol Elizabeth Heiss   110
Joan Joyce   112
Billy Jean Moffitt King   115
Julie Krone   118
Andrea Mead Lawrence   122
Nancy Lopez   125
Patricia Keller McCormick
128
Rosi Mittermeier   131
Martina Navratilova   135
Diana Nyad   138

Annemarie Moser-Proell   142
Wilma Glodean Rudolph
145
Lydia Skoblikova   148
Irena Kirszenstein
Szewinska   150
Wyomia Tyus   153
Grete Anderson Waitz
156
Kathryne Ann Whitworth
159
Katarina Witt   162
Mary Kathryn Wright   165
Sheila Grace Young   168

Appendix: The Greatest Woman Athlete of All Time   173
Index   175

Preface

Great women athletes? There are many. Most of them had to overcome a great deal to achieve stardom. This book tells about 50 great women athletes and contains three sections:

The Top Five
The Pioneers
Thirty-five More Great Women Athletes

The "top five" are the opinion of the author. It is difficult to compare athletes of one era with those of another, so the judgments are subjective. The five were selected because they either (1) dominated a sport for a decade or more, (2) competed successfully in several sports, or (3) established the standards by which later competitors are judged.

The "pioneers" are a virtually forgotten group of people, yet they were all great athletes, the stars of their day, and made breakthroughs that have since been taken for granted.

The third section, "Thirty-five More Great Women Athletes," is that and no more. Certainly other great ones—Robyn Smith, Janet Guthrie, Debbie Meyer and Kristin Otto—come to mind, but when athletes of this caliber are omitted, one realizes just how many great women athletes there have been.

The author is a father of six and grandfather of six. He teaches Computer Information Systems at Westchester Community College and fancies himself a sports historian.

He feels that, if any athlete has done remarkable things, people should have the opportunity to read about them. Especially those athletes about whom not enough has been written.

Introduction: Women in Sports

The Ancient World

Athletes have competed in sporting events since before the beginning of recorded history. Ancient literature abounds with references to wrestling and boxing matches, throwing contests, and foot, horse, and chariot races. There is virtually no mention of women participating in these activities; in fact, they were seldom welcome as spectators. The ancient Olympic games were "for men only." The only woman present at the festivities was the priestess of Demeter, who sat in a place of honor. Any other woman found in the arena was escorted to a nearby cliff and thrown to her death.

Greek athletes usually competed without clothing; the word "gymnasium" is derived from the Greek word for naked. One story is that the male athletes originally wore loincloths while competing, but one athlete accidentally lost his and went on to win the race. Others soon followed suit. Another theory used to explain naked competition is that the men wanted to be sure no woman sneaked into the races to show them up.

Young girls of Sparta were allowed to train and participate in sports, but the practice was ridiculed in most of the other Greek city-states. The Spartans believed that physical activity enabled women to bear stronger sons who would grow to become better warriors. Women competed in the Heraean Games in honor of Hera, Zeus's wife, the queen of the gods. Sixteen women of various ages did some running in these games as part of a festival honoring the goddess. The event was a religious ceremony as much as an athletic contest.

Some evidence exists that women participated in chariot races later in the Hellenic Period, first as horse owners and later as participants. Women seldom competed during the period of Roman domination although they were frequently spectators at athletic contests.

The Greek and Roman eras were male-dominated times. One of the prizes for winning a chariot race mentioned in ancient literature was "a woman skilled in women's work." Although women gained some freedom in the latter days of the ancient world, they were never equal in status to men. Thucydides, writing in the fifth century B.C., summed up the prevailing attitude towards women in these words: "It is your great glory . . . not to be talked about by men at all, neither for praise nor blame."

Sports Through the Centuries

The relationship between sports and war preparation always existed. The history of the Middle Ages abounds with stories of jousts, duels, and archery contests. The English-speaking world grew up on tales of Arthur's brave knights and of Robin Hood. But only men of noble birth were privileged to engage in these contests. The masses did not have the leisure time to participate in active sport, nor the wherewithal to afford the equipment. Since women did not participate in war, with the notable exception of Joan of Arc, there was no need for them to "get into shape." It would seem the term "sportsmanship" was not coined by accident.

Sport probably became formalized around 1750 when structured physical activities were added to the syllabi of Europe's military schools. Sporting events grew in number as free time increased. People have always played with a ball; sometimes they kicked it or hit it with a stick, occasionally they threw it or tucked it under their arm and ran with it. When these activities were organized and rules drawn up, a sport was born. Golf traces its roots to Scotland in the 1100s. Mary Queen of Scots played golf in 1567, hitting a pellet filled with chicken feathers. She was the exception for women were next recorded playing golf in 1867 when a women's golf club was established at St. Andrews in Scotland. As late as 1894, one British fashion magazine proclaimed "except for putting," golf was "not a game for ladies."

The few sports that women participated in historically developed during the nineteenth century. Archery has been a popular sport in the Western world for centuries, and it is said that Queen Victoria was excellent with the bow. Of course it was a sport of the rich and titled, but one in which both men and women could compete. Although it was normally contested without formalized records until quite recently, archery for women was an unofficial sport at the 1904 Olympics in St. Louis where an American, Lydia Scott Howell, won three gold medals. She was a national champion seventeen times between 1882 and 1907.

Bowling also has been played in one form or another for centuries. Even today no neighborhood in Italy is without its bocci court where men gather to play, usually well out of the sight of women. The Dutch bowled on the green on lower Manhattan Island in the early 1600s. In the United States more women participate in bowling than any other sport. The Women's International Bowling Congress numbers more than 4 million members. The industrial leagues that developed after World War II popularized the sport among blue collar workers, providing healthy exercise for both men and women.

Fencing developed from the deadly act of dueling but became a fashionable sport for women as early as the 1880s. Fencing for women became an Olympic sport in 1924.

Women ice-skated in the cities of Boston and New York in the nineteenth century. It was strictly a social pastime until Sonja Henie performed at such a level of excellence that today it is one of the few sports in which women athletes create more interest than the men.

The rules of lawn tennis were formalized in England in 1875, although tennis was played there for decades prior to that. An annual championship tournament was soon initiated at Wimbledon and by 1884 included women's matches. European women were well ahead of the Americans in becoming active in tennis. As early as 1879, the Fitzwilliam Club in Ireland held an Irish tennis championship that included women's singles and mixed doubles competition. The game was introduced in the United States by Mary Outerbridge, a Staten Island socialite, who saw it played in Bermuda. The first tennis court in the country was set up at the Staten Island Cricket and Baseball Club in 1874, and within a few years people of society were playing at Tuxedo Park, New York, and Newport, Rhode Island. May Sutton was the first great American champion and a two-time winner at Wimbledon.

The United States in the Nineteenth Century

Two factors greatly hampered the development of women's sports in the United States. First, the original New England settlers considered all sports frivolous and participation by women immoral. Second, Victorian thinking, imported from nineteenth-century England, put women on a pedestal. Women were expected to be frail, pale, and at home.

One of the first breakthroughs for women in sports occurred in New Orleans in 1851 when women were first allowed into a United States racetrack as spectators. They were confined to a special ladies' grandstand, however, and did not mingle with the men. One lesson was learned; having women present improved behavior at sporting events. The little athletic activity that existed for women in the United States before 1880 was noncompetitive and informal. In the South and West women rode horses and sometimes participated in the hunt. Annie Oakley could use a rifle as well as any man. In the East women played croquet, the most popular participation sport among both men and women during the second half of the nineteenth century.

Some opportunities for women athletes of that era arose in the development of the safety bicycle and the acceptance in women's schools of Amelia Bloomer's gym suit. The need for comfortable recreational clothing has plagued women throughout the history of sports. When Miss Bloomer, an early feminist, designed her costume for physical activities in the 1850s many were aghast. Immediately, however, sporting activities were introduced at the women's colleges, where the most influential women of that era attended school. The bicycle became a craze in the 1880s and 1890s, especially after "Mile-a-Minute" Kelley rode a bicycle at 60 miles per hour behind a train on a specially constructed board track on Long Island. The bicycle was a safe means of exercise for women and gave both sexes an opportunity to get away to socialize, far from peering eyes. No wonder couples of the 1890s sang about Daisy on her "bicycle built for two."

The Scottish game of golf was first played in the United States in November of 1888 at a six-hole course laid out by John Reid in Yonkers, New York. The course later became the St. Andrews Golf Club, now located in Hastings-on-Hudson, New York. Although St. Andrews became a men's-only club, on March 20, 1889, John Reid, his wife, John Upham, and Miss Carrie Law formed a foursome to play the Yonkers course. Within a few years women's courses were developed at Southampton on Long Island; Morristown, New Jersey, and Evanston, Illinois, but they did not survive. The first women's amateur championship was played at the Meadow Brook Club at Hempstead, Long Island, in 1895.

Women's participation in other sports was equally limited. Men and women got together to play croquet and participated in archery. Women played college basketball in 1892, the year after the game was invented. Other women bowled or took fencing lessons. Women who ice-skated were considered hussies because a fall might reveal a stockinged ankle or, worse yet, a leg. Few women could swim before the turn of the century. The Boston YWCA was ahead of its time when it held some track and field events in the 1880s and volleyball a few years later.

Eastern women's colleges fostered intramural physical activities and sports during the second half of the nineteenth century. Mount Holyoke, Vassar, Mills, Wellesley and Smith college students were involved in croquet, bowling, archery, tennis, horseback riding, and walking before 1880. These activities were held in the school gymnasium or on its playing fields and were not intended for men's eyes. Ironically, there was an attempt to organize a women's professional baseball league as early as 1890. W. S. Franklin of New York failed in his attempt to put the league together, possibly because he required that his players be less than 20 years old and "possess good looks and a good figure." The prevailing attitude regarding women athletics at the turn of the twentieth century might have been summed up in an excerpt from a 1901 article entitled "The Athletic Girl": "The aim of athletics among women has been the establishment and maintenance of a high general standard of health and vigor, rather than some single brilliant achievement."

At least it was a start.

The Olympic Movement

The modern Olympics were first conducted in 1896 for male athletes. One woman requested to run in the 26-mile marathon, but the founder of the modern Olympics, Baron Pierre de Coubertin, saw to it that the application was denied, saying, "It is indecent that the spectators should be exposed to the risk of seeing the body of a woman being smashed before their eyes . . . her organism is not cut out to sustain certain shocks." The woman ran unofficially and finished.

The 1900 and 1904 Olympic games in Paris and St. Louis were haphazardly organized as sideshows for international exhibitions. Women competed "unofficially" in golf, tennis, and archery.

Women first officially competed at the 1908 Olympics in both individual and pairs skating, conducted in those days during the summer festival. Swimming and diving were added in 1912; track and field in 1928. There were four track-and-field events for women in 1928: a 100-meter dash won by Elizabeth Robinson of the United States; a 4×100-meter relay won by Canada; a high jump, won by Canadian Ethyl Catherwood, and the 800-meter run—which set the cause of women's distance running back 30 years. Although the winner, Lina Radke of Germany established a world record that stood for 16 years, several of the participants were totally unprepared for the distance and collapsed along the way or after the finish. As a result, the International Amateur Athletic Federation limited women's races to 200 meters, a rule that held at the Olympics until 1960.

Since 1932 Olympic competition produced a woman superstar virtually every time the games were conducted. It was Babe Didrikson in 1932, Sonja Henie in 1936, and a Dutch housewife, Fanny Blankers-Koen, who stole the show in 1948. In more recent times the Games have made household names of Wilma Rudolph, Peggy Fleming, Katerina Witt, and Florence Joyner.

The Twentieth Century

Women made little progress in sports for the first two decades because of the clothing society demanded they wear. They shot their arrows, retrieved tennis lobs and teed their golf balls, ever mindful not to reveal an ankle, or even an arm. There were good players in those days in golf and tennis, the two sports that were considered feminine, but clothing greatly hampered their game. Lottie Dod, the first woman "super athlete," who was a multiple winner at Wimbledon, a British national golf champion, and an Olympic medal winner in archery, said, "Hearty indeed would be the thanks of puzzled lady players to the individual who invented an easy and pretty costume." Marie Wagner, an American tennis star of that era, added, "No girl would appear unless upholstered with a corset, a starched petticoat, a starched skirt, heavily button-trimmed blouse, a starched shirtwaist with long sleeves and cuff links, a high collar and four-in-hand necktie, a belt with silver buckle, and sneakers with large silk bows."

Track-and-field meets for women were probably first held in Germany in 1904. The first recorded women's world record in track and field was produced by American E. MacBeth, who ran 50 yards in six seconds flat. Records for women swimmers were first recorded in 1908. Lula Gill was the first woman jockey to win a horse race in 1906.

The woman athlete emerged in the 1920s. Women in the United States could finally vote and celebrated their newly found freedom of movement dancing the "Charleston." It was a wacky, wild era, but one that allowed people to do their thing. At stately old Wimbledon, a saucy French player, Suzanne Lenglen, was peerless on the tennis court and a style-setter both on the court and off who believed that a person should be comfortable while playing a sport. Suzanne was a great tennis player and attracted lasting recognition to the game of women's tennis, along with American Helen Wills Moody.

The 1920s was the golden era of sports in the United States. People recognized Babe Ruth, Jack Dempsey, Red Grange, Bobby Jones, and Bill Tilden more readily than the three Presidents of the decade, Warren Harding, Calvin Coolidge, and Herbert Hoover. Gertrude Ederle, a butcher's daughter, swam the English Channel in 1926 and returned to a ticker tape parade seen by 2 million. Helen Wills, the beautiful and intelligent "Little Miss Poker Face," became the queen of tennis. They both won international acclaim as great athletes, and hardly anyone made a fuss over the fact that they were women.

Two stars dominated women's sports in the 1930s, the versatile and colorful Babe Didrikson Zaharias and the moody "ice queen" from Norway, Sonja Henie. When they had to leave amateur competition to earn a living Didrikson became a national treasure and Henie a glamorous movie star. Yet women were not as accepted in sports in the 1930s as during the 1920s. One reason was an active and effective lobbying campaign against women in sports led by several church and women's groups and spearheaded by the first lady, Lou Hoover. Lack of finances was another reason. There was little money for sports development when a large part of the working force was on the breadline.

The second half of the twentieth century has seen a revolution in women's sports that is still unfolding. The world changed dramatically as a result of World War II. Western Europe, where women competed in a variety of sports throughout the century, produced the first woman superstar of the postwar period when Blankers-Koen, a 30-year-old mother of two, ran away with most of the laurels at the 1948 Olympic games. In Eastern Europe, Soviet bloc nations found that sports was a means of propagandizing the socialist state. Athletes were methodically developed, and the Soviets, Czechs, and East German athletic machines produced many of the world's finest athletes. Women were frequently the stars of these national teams. Soviet track athletes and East German swimmers became state heroes. In the United States, women excelled in their own world of professional golf for the first time soon after World War II. The Ladies Professional Golf Association was formed around two marquee names, Patty Berg and Didrikson Zaharias. Women athletes flourished in tennis, softball, basketball, volleyball, skiing, and skating. But lack of money and facilities hampered development of these programs.

The postwar period also marked the emergence of great Australian women athletes, led by Beth Cuthbert, a three-gold-medal Olympian in track and field, and all-time greats, swimmer Dawn Fraser and tennis star Margaret Smith Court.

Two factors joined to promote women's athletics—Title IX funding in American colleges and the demise of amateurism. Title IX of the Educational Amendments of 1972 reads: "No person in the United States shall, on the basis of sex, be excluded from participation in, be denied the benefits of, or be subjected to discrimination under any educational program or activity receiving federal financial assistance."

Title IX created college athletic scholarships for women. Evaluating its effectiveness is beyond the scope of this book. It may mean that a girl who is an outstanding high school soccer player may have the same opportunity for scholarship money as an outstanding boy soccer player. The immediate result was the increase in the number of women in collegiate competition from about 8000 in 1967 to more than 60,000 in 1974. But for a variety of reasons, one of which being that no collegiate women's sports activity fills a 100,000-seat stadium or brings in lofty television revenue, the total amount of women's scholarship money has not yet equaled the men's.

Money has always been an issue in women's sports. During the 1970s open competition was initiated in tennis and golf, and amateur competition at the big-time level disappeared. Men continued receiving more prize money than women. Bobby Riggs pronounced that it was because "they play a better game," so when Riggs was defeated by Billy Jean King in the much-heralded "Battle of the Sexes" in 1973 it opened the way for women to earn a reasonable living in sports. For a brief period, women's team competition flourished. Professional leagues in softball, tennis, and basketball were organized; financial pressures forced each of these leagues out of business. At this writing, the only professional team–sport league for women athletes exists in volleyball. In fact, of the 50 women discussed in this book, only one, Joan Joyce, made her reputation in a team sport.

Although women's team sports have not caught on, the woman professional athlete is doing well in the 1990s because of corporate sponsors. Mary Decker would have had to retire if she were competing 30 years ago; today she can raise a family, continue to run in her 30s, and command a six-figure income. Florence Joyner and Katarina Witt are popular personalities, and swimmers who used to retire at age 17, now can devote the time required to compete internationally and still pay the bills.

Few could anticipate the changes that have taken place in women's sports, yet an editorial in the July 16, 1877, New York *Daily Graphic* prophetically stated:

> A few years ago the delightful game of croquet was welcomed by the ladies, and soon became the fashion. It led the way to another out of door sport for ladies, and last week we reported the formation of an athletic club for practice of archery and other field sports by ladies on Staten Island. The tendency is a good one and ought to be heartily encouraged. . . . And athletic sports will become fashionable for ladies as well as for men . . . and many sports which a few years ago were considered unwomanly will doubtless be fashionable.

The Top Five

Babe Didrikson also excelled in swimming and diving as well as in her better-known sports, golf and track and field (photo courtesy Lamar University).

Mildred Ella Didrikson Zaharias

"The Texas Babe"
June 26, 1911–September 27, 1956
Port Arthur, Texas

Babe Didrikson could do it all. Only Jim Thorpe has surpassed her athletic versatility. Babe was a natural, yet she worked hard to perfect her varied skills.

Mildred Didrikson started in organized sports as a basketball player. She was employed by the Employers Casualty Insurance Company of Dallas before the end of her senior year in high school, secondarily as a typist; primarily as a basketball player. Women's college sports generally did not exist during the 1930s, and girl's high school competition was limited. The better women competitors had one real option. They could represent the companies for which they worked. Only two American woman athletes had achieved national stature: English Channel swimmer Gertrude Ederle and tennis star Helen Wills.

Didrikson was a phenomenon on the basketball court. In an era when men's teams scored 25 points per game, Babe averaged 42 points a game to lead Employers Casualty to the 1930 Amateur Athletic Union (AAU) women's championship. That year the company started a track team. Babe joined, although she had no prior track experience. Within a year, she was the best woman track athlete in Texas; by 1932 she was the best in the world.

On July 16, 1932, Babe Didrikson accomplished an athletic feat that will never be duplicated. She was the only member of the Employers Casualty track team to enter the AAU Nationals, yet she single-handedly won the women's track team championship. Babe scored 30 points; the Illinois Women's Athletic Club was second with 22, and San Francisco's Western Women's Club was a distant third with 13. The one-woman "team" in one day won the 80-meter hurdles, baseball throw, long jump, shot put, and javelin throw. She tied for first in a sixth event, the high jump.

Didrikson earned her reputation as the finest woman athlete in the world in the 1932 Olympics in Los Angeles. She won gold medals in the 80-meter hurdles and javelin throw. She tied for first place in the high jump, but was placed second because her head preceded her torso as she jumped, a common technique today but illegal in 1932.

Since women could earn no money in athletic competition, and Babe had to support herself and help out at home, she joined the vaudeville circuit. Her act featured running on a treadmill, hitting plastic golf balls, and playing the harmonica, which she did quite well. Babe also traveled with a men's barnstorming baseball team, the House of David, pitching an inning or two at every whistle stop in the country. She toured with a coed basketball team during the winter. Since these activities made her a professional, she was ineligible to compete in amateur sports and was not a member of the 1936 United States Olympic team.

But Didrikson's athletic career was far from over. During the late 1930s, Babe Didrikson, now married to former wrestler and sports promoter George Zaharias, applied for reinstatement as an amateur to compete in tennis and golf. Although she could play tennis with the very best in the country, she was never allowed to compete because tennis officials followed the principle, "once a professional, always a professional." Her amateur golf eligibility was restored after she sat out eight seasons.

As an amateur for two years in 1946 and 1947 she won 17 consecutive tournaments, including the United States Amateur in 1946 and the British Amateur in 1947. She was the first American woman to win the British title. The Ladies Professional Golf Association was formed in 1948 with Didrikson Zaharias the primary attraction. Babe won the United States Women's Open championship in 1948, 1950, and 1954; in 1954, she won the Vare Trophy for the lowest average score for that year's competition. Babe competed professionally for eight years and won 31 LPGA tournaments.

After voting her "Woman Athlete of the Year" five times, the Associated Press in 1950 named her the "Greatest Female Athlete of the First Half of the 20th Century."

Babe was brash, confident, and gutsy; as a young competitor her bragging annoyed many, but she mellowed as she matured and became a national heroine and pioneer for women's professional sports. President Dwight Eisenhower was among her personal friends. Colon cancer first struck Babe in 1953, and she was told that her golfing career was finished. But she rallied to again beat the odds—and all opponents at the 1954 United States Women's Open to win by 12 strokes. She died of cancer in 1956.

Track and golf immortal, basketball great, swimmer, diver, baseball player, pool enthusiast and harmonica player . . . Didrikson, without a doubt, was the greatest all-around woman athlete of her (or any other) half century.

Dawn Fraser

"Free Spirit"
September 4, 1937–
Balmain, New South Wales, Australia

Dawn Fraser frequently displayed the free spirit and disregard for regulations that Australians thrive upon. Amateur officials could not cope with her. Australians loved her, especially since she was the finest woman swimmer ever.

She won the 100-meter freestyle swim at the 1956, 1960, and 1964 Olympics, the only swimmer to take a gold medal at three consecutive Olympiads. In the 400-meters she was second, fifth, and fourth, respectively, at the three summer games and contributed to seven medals on relay teams, four of them gold.

In 1956, Fraser established a world record of 1:02.0 for 100 meters during the Olympics when she nosed out fellow–Australian, Lorraine Crapp. The previous record had been established in 1936. She remained undefeated at 100 meters for the four years leading up to the 1960 Games at Rome. There she defeated American Chris Von Saltza in the finals to establish a new Olympic record of 1:01.2. That record fell in 1964 when the Australian needed only 59.5 seconds to defeat Sharon Stouder for gold in the 100 meters.

During her colorful ten-year career, Fraser set 27 world records and broke the world record for 100 meters nine times. Her 58.9 recorded at North Sydney in February of 1964 lasted until 1972 when it was broken by Shane Gould. She was the first woman to break the one-minute barrier for both 100 meters and 110 yards. In addition to her Olympic accomplishments, the athlete garnered six gold and two silver medals at the British Commonwealth Games and 23 Australian national titles: seven at 100 meters, eight at 200 meters, five at 400 meters, two in the 100-meter butterfly and one in the 200-meter medley relay.

Dawn Fraser was born in Balmain, a working-class suburb of Sydney, the youngest of eight children. Overcoming two serious tragedies perhaps inspired her to greatness. When she was a teenager, her brother and first swimming teacher, Don, died of leukemia at the age of 21. Then in March of 1964, when Dawn was 26, the car she was driving crashed into a parked truck, killing her mother. Dawn chipped a vertebra in her neck in the crash but within six months enjoyed her astounding third Olympic feats.

Dawn's first bout with Australian swimming officials was at the 1960

Dawn Fraser, a great swimmer and one of the most colorful personalities in sports (photo courtesy International Swimming Hall of Fame).

Olympics in Rome when she was asked at the last minute to swim a leg on a relay team. She had spent the previous evening celebrating her successful defense of the 100-meter title with much pasta and red wine. At the time she was asked she had just downed a bowl of spaghetti. She was not ready to swim and said so. Fraser was shunned by team members and officials for her refusal.

When Dawn became the first woman to break one minute for the 100-meter free-style at the 1962 British Commonwealth Games in Melbourne, she again incurred the wrath of team officials. After registering her 59.9 milestone a reporter asked how she would celebrate her breakthrough. "Have a beer. Probably get tight," she playfully answered.

So the Australian officials were pushed over the limit in 1964 in Tokyo, when their star swimmer was arrested for stealing a souvenir Japanese flag from the grounds of the Emperor's palace. The offender Dawn herself described the incident as "a chase that would have delighted Mack Sennett. It involved the theft of a policeman's bicycle, a romp around the Emperor's shrubs, and an unsuccessful attempt to swim the palace moat." The police released her, but Australian Swimming Union officials were not so forgiving. They banned her from competition for ten years for that sin and for participating in the Olympic Opening Day Ceremonies against the orders of the Australian officials.

Most Australians thoroughly enjoyed the tempest and undoubtedly wished they could have joined the flag-stealing sortie. Dawn Fraser was selected "Australian of the Year" for 1964 by the Australian Day Council.

After her enforced retirement in 1965, Dawn married a legal bookmaker, Gary Ware, and had one daughter. The couple subsequently separated. The suspension from competition was lifted in 1968, but at age 30 she realized it was too late for a return to international competition. Australian swimming officials were likely relieved by her decision more than disappointed by the loss of potential medals.

Sonja Henie
"The Pavlova of the Ice"
April 8, 1912–October 13, 1969
Oslo, Norway

On February 18, 1928, the *New York Times* routinely reported the results of the Olympic figure-skating competition: "The defeat of Miss Beatrix Loughran

The incomparable Sonja Henie, three-time Olympic gold medalist (photo courtesy World Figure Skating Museum).

of New York, popular favorite to win the women's figure skating title, provided the chief sensation of the Olympic Winter sports program today. The judges' decision announced late tonight, awarded the figure skating title to Miss Henie, a 16-year-old Norwegian girl. . . ." The correspondent had no idea he was announcing the coming-of-age of a sport in which women would excel.

Henie was placed first by all eight Olympic judges and was instantly a world-wide celebrity. Women's figure skating has evolved through three phases: Recently, Katarina Witt showed the world how to interpret music on ice. Before her, Peggy Fleming demonstrated that ice skating can be as beautiful as ballet. Sonja Henie taught the world to skate. The others refined the sport; she defined it.

Henie was not the prototypical athlete. A petite, five-foot-two-inch, 105-pound bundle of energy, this blond with the button nose and dimples had fabulous careers as an athlete and a movie actress. But it was her sophisticated style that revolutionized figure skating and her ability to charm skating audiences that established the sport both in North America and Europe.

Sonja Henie was born in Oslo, Norway, in 1912, the daughter of wealthy, sport-minded parents. Her father, Wilhelm, operated the largest furrier business in Europe; her mother's family operated a fleet of lumber-carrying vessels. Wilhelm was a world-class cyclist who won the world bicycling championship twice and was nationally known in skiing and skating. Mrs. Henie was an important influence in Sonja's athletic development. She recognized Sonja's natural grace and hoped that she would become a prima ballerina. Sonja had her first ballet lessons when she was two. Although she never danced at the great theaters of Europe, ballet strongly influenced her skating.

Miss Henie won her first skating competition as a five-year-old speedskater, and by the time she was eight she was unbeatable in age-group figure skating. Already ballet movements set apart this youngster from the stiff movement considered good form by her contemporaries. Her style was 50 years ahead of its time. Sonja won the Norwegian women's figure-skating title in 1923 when she was ten and qualified for the first Winter Olympics in Charmonix, France, in early 1924. She finished eighth and last; never again was she defeated in ice-skating competition. She won the world's figure-skating championship in 1927 as a 14-year-old, her first of ten consecutive world titles. Perhaps the judges could not resist her ballet style and pretty smile, both of which were highlighted by a white silk and ermine costume featuring a short skirt. She was the world champion from 1927 until 1936, the year she turned professional. Sonja was known universally as the "Pavlova of the ice."

Sonja Henie's record in major competition from 1923 until 1936, when she turned professional at the age of 34, is shown below. The blanks represent events which were either not held, or in which she did not compete.

YEAR		Championship Won		
1923	Norwegian			
1924	Norwegian			
1925	Norwegian			
1926	Norwegian			
1927	Norwegian	World		
1928	Norwegian	World	European	Olympic
1929	Norwegian	World	European	

YEAR		Championship Won	
1930	World	European	
1931	World	European	
1932	World	European	Olympic
1933	World	European	
1934	World	European	
1935	World	European	
1936	World	European	Olympic

Sonja also won the Norwegian doubles title three times with partner Arne Lie.

Sonja Henie was unbeatable in Olympic competition, winning in 1928 at St. Moritz, 1932 at Lake Placid, and 1936 at Garmisch-Partenkirchen, each time by large margins. She won the Norwegian national championship each of the seven years in which she competed. In addition to her skating skills, Henie was Norway's third-ranked woman tennis player and was an outstanding swimmer, equestrienne, and ballet dancer.

Asked to name the finest woman figure skater of all time, Dick Button answered, "If I had to name one, it would be Sonja Henie. She had the most distinguished competitive career and she clearly affected the sport more than anyone before or after." Sandra Stevenson of the Manchester Guardian adds, "She revolutionized the sport, changing it from an amusing pastime engaged in by the upper classes in the elite winter watering spots to a highly competitive, actively contested sport."

After the 1936 Olympics Henie turned professional and toured in her own ice show. Her "Hollywood Reviews" played regularly at New York's Madison Square Garden until 1952. One reviewer wrote, "She gave the United States ice-skating fever." But her driving ambition was to be a movie star: "I want to go into pictures and I want to do well. I want to do with skates what Fred Astaire is doing with dancing. No one has ever done it in the movies, and I want to."

The opportunity quickly came and a skater became America's sweetheart in the late 1930s; by the early 1940s she was one of Hollywood's top box office draws. Her first movie, "One in a Million," costarring Don Ameche and the Ritz Brothers, was a 1937 box office smash. In another 11 films Henie costarred with Tyrone Power, Cesar Romero, Ethyl Merman, Buddy Ebsen, Arthur Treacher, Rudy Vallee, Ray Milland, Robert Cummings, John Payne, Milton Berle, Jack Oakie, Carole Landis, and Marie McDonald. The critics praised her skating and panned her acting. The theater-going public lined up at the box office for every film in which she was featured.

Sonja Henia made over $50 million during her skating and movie careers. She lived the life of a movie queen, collecting jewelry, furs, and fine art. She was married three times—to Americans Dan Topping, the sports tycoon, and socialite Winthrop Gardiner, and to Norwegian shipping magnate, Niels Oustad. Her art collection and personal jewels are currently in an Oslo museum she founded. She succumbed to leukemia on October 12, 1969.

For all practical purposes, Sonja Henie invented the sport of ice skating as it is known today. Her consistency in competition and the margin by which she dominated her contemporaries has not been approached by any other figure skater.

Jacqueline Joyner-Kersee
"Dreams and Goals"
March 3, 1962–
East St. Louis, Illinois

Only track-and-field aficionados keep track of winners in women's pentathlon championships. A competitor must excel at the World Games or the Olympics to receive recognition. Jackie Joyner-Kersee has done both and, although she is acclaimed as the finest woman athlete in the world at this writing, Joyner-Kersee is relatively unknown.

Ironically, most experts agree that Joyner-Kersee ranks second only to Babe Didrikson Zaharias as the finest woman athlete who ever competed. Even while she was establishing herself as the world's greatest woman athlete during the 1988 Olympics, her accomplishments were overshadowed by the flamboyant running style of her sister-in-law, Florence Griffith-Joyner. Her success in the 1988 Olympic games was down-played because it was assumed that she was unbeatable in the women's long jump and a cinch to win any seven-event heptathlon. Joyner-Kersee is so good an athlete that people take her for granted, despite the hard work required to achieve her level of performance.

Jackie Joyner was born in East St. Louis, Illinois, an impoverished town across the Mississippi River from St. Louis, Missouri. She was the second of four children in a family she describes as "having a lot of loving and caring." Her father was a construction worker and railroad switch operator and her mother a practical nurse. When Jackie was born, her mom was 17, and her dad 19, and they had been married for three years. The family was poor and East St. Louis was a grim place to grow up. One writer described the Joyner's house as "little more than wallpaper and sticks."

Jackie Joyner started competing in track when she was nine, and was long jumping over 17 feet before age 13. She won the National Junior Pentathlon championship at 14, a title she successfully defended three times. Her older brother Al was so inspired by his sister's success that he took up track and was good enough to win the Olympic gold medal in the triple jump in 1984. Jackie was a fine student; she finished tenth in her high school class and was the best female basketball player in the state, earning a basketball scholarship to UCLA in 1979.

Joyner's days at UCLA were happy and successful, except that her mother died of meningitis at the age of 38 during her freshman year. Jackie Joyner maintained a B average while majoring in history and communications, starred in basketball and track and field, and met her husband-to-be, Bob Kersee, a coach of UCLA's women's track team. The couple proved to be a winning combination. It was Bob who convinced his wife that she could be a world-class competitor in multi-event competition. She qualified for the Olympic team as a long jumper in 1980, but the American boycott of the games prevented her from competing.

In 1982, Jackie won the National Collegiate Athletic Association (NCAA) heptathlon championship, where she was called the "finest female athlete in college competition." The heptathlon consists of seven events: 100-meter hurdles, high jump, shot put, 200-meter dash, long jump, javelin throw, and 800-meter run. Jackie qualified for the 1984 United States Olympic team in the heptathlon and won the silver medal at Los Angeles. Glynis Nunn, an Australian, nosed her out for the gold by a few steps in the 800-meter run (Joyner-Kersee actually missed the gold medal by .3 seconds which translates into five points). She was only beginning to mature as an athlete, however.

Joyner-Kersee set a world record in the heptathlon at the Goodwill Games in Moscow in 1986, with a score of 7148 points—which made a shambles of the 7000-point barrier and was 200 points better than the old record. She broke this record three weeks later. She won the prestigious Sullivan Award as the nation's outstanding amateur athlete that year. In 1987, Joyner-Kersee began concentrating on an unusual double, the pentathlon and the long jump. She won both events at the 1987 Pan American Games and at the 1988 World Games in Rome. She established a new world record for the pentathlon at the 1988 Olympic trials and her career peaked that September when she easily won the gold medal in the pentathlon and long jump at the Seoul Olympics. Her Olympic pentathlon performance:

Event	Performance	Points	Comment
100-meter hurdles	12.69	1172	personal best
high jump	6-1 1/2	1054	injured knee, best was 6-4

Jackie Joyner-Kersee, the finest woman athlete alive (photo courtesy Amateur Athletic Union).

Event	Performance	Points	Comment
shot put	51-10	915	personal best
200-meter dash	22.56	1123	almost personal best
long jump	23-10 1/4	1264	Olympic heptathlon record
javelin throw	149-10	776	
800-meter run	2:08.5	987	

By the time Jackie reached the last event, the 800-meter run, she had compiled such a lead that she could almost have walked and retained first place. In the long jump, she deliberately jumped off the wrong foot to save a tender knee injured in the high jump and still set an Olympic heptathlon record. Her total of 7291 points was nearly 400 points better than the runner-up, Sabine John, of East Germany. She went on to defeat the world record holder in the open long jump to win a second gold medal.

In the pentathlon Joyner-Kersee is the only person to top 7000 points in the event, and she has done it five times. Along the way she won the Jesse Owens Award as the nation's outstanding track-and-field athlete in 1986 and 1987 and was runner-up to her sister-in-law, Florence Griffith-Joyner, in 1988. She also won McDonald's Amateur Sportsperson of the Year Award in 1987.

Joyner-Kersee is five feet, ten inches, tall and weighs 153 pounds. She hopes for a career in television when she finishes competing. She once said, "I only dreamed of being the best I could be." That happens to be the best in the world today in what she does. She also tries to pass on that dream: "I remember where I came from. If young girls see the environment I grew up in, and my dreams and goals came true, they will realize that their dreams and goals might also come true."

Helen Wills Moody

"Little Miss Poker Face"
October 6, 1905–
Berkeley, California

During the 1920s, the "Golden Age of Sports," the finest woman athlete was tennis star Helen Wills. New York sportswriter, W. O. McGeehan, labeled her "Little Miss Poker Face," and she worked hard to earn the sobriquet. She was a devastating competitor.

Wills was taught the game by her father, a doctor in Berkeley, California,

Helen Wills (right) greets Suzanne Lenglen before their famous 1926 match (photo courtesy of Wide World Photos).

and tennis fans first heard of her in 1921 when she won the 18-Year-Old Girls' Singles at Forest Hills. There Helen Wills first saw the reigning queen of tennis, Suzanne Lenglen of France, who won the open Women's Singles title at that tournament: "She impressed me, especially when I saw her with six rackets. I knew what kind of tennis I intended to play." That "kind of tennis" dominated an era, and some experts still consider Helen Wills to be the finest woman tennis player of all time.

Wills won the United States Women's Singles title six times between 1923 and 1931 and won eight singles titles at Wimbledon, her last in 1938 at age

33. She also won four doubles titles at Forest Hills and three at Wimbledon. She won the French Open four times and played ten times in Wightman Cup competition against Great Britain's best. With an overall record of 18-2. During her career, she played Suzanne Lenglen only once, in a much-heralded match held at the plush Carlton Club in Cannes, France, in 1926. Lenglen won the two sets, 6–2, 8–6, but the day was not a total loss. In the midst of the post-match milling, Freedy Moody, a San Francisco stockbroker, proposed to her, and the couple married in 1929. An attack of appendicitis kept Wills from a rematch with Lenglen at Wimbledon that year, and Lenglen turned professional before they had another opportunity to compete.

At her peak, Helen Wills Moody was literally unbeatable. From 1927 until 1932 she never lost a *set* in competition, let alone a match. In that stretch she won five Wimbledon, four United States and four French National titles. From August 1926 until 1935 she never lost a match anywhere in the world. She defeated the other great player of that era, Helen Jacobs, in 14 of the 15 matches they played, including all four times in Wimbledon finals. Jacobs was no slouch; she won the United States Singles Championship four times and Wimbledon once. In the 1924 Olympics Wills defeated Julie Vlasto of France 6–2, 6–2 to win the women's finals. She also teamed with Hazel Wightman to win the gold medal in the women's doubles. Tennis was discontinued as an Olympic sport from 1924 until 1988.

Wills Moody was tough with the pressure on. In the nine times she appeared in the United States Singles finals she lost only twice (her first and last appearances).

On the court she was a machine, emotionless as she mercilessly cut her opponents down. But the stoic facade hid a burning desire to excel. She had less natural skill than many of the great players, but intense practice enabled her to hit the ball harder than many men of her day, and her composure under fire and fierce desire to win made her an all-time great. The possibility of defeat never occurred to her.

With the reputation of being a human icicle, she was never the darling of the galleries. There was neither Lenglen's ballerina-like grace nor the winning smile of Jacobs. She was great but dull. At her first appearance at Wimbledon she wore her school uniform: middy blouse, black tie, and pleated skirt. Except for adding the green and white visor that became her trademark, she seldom varied the outfit throughout her career.

Although Americans called her "Our Helen," she received warmer receptions from the British, to whom she was "Queen Helen." Off the court she was intelligent, beautiful, and urbane. Paul Gallico, in the glowing terms of 1920 sportswriting, called her "regally beautiful, insuperably efficient, calm, cold, ruthless, implacable, dignified, aloof, ambitious, imperious, successful."

Unlike most fine athletes, sports was only a small part of her life. She seldom spoke to the press and socialized infrequently with fellow tennis players. She lunched with Lady Astor, supped with George Bernard Shaw, and was presented to Queen Mary at Buckingham Palace. No wonder the British loved her. Helen was a fine painter who, while at the peak of her tennis success in 1929, exhibited drawings and water-color paintings in London and New York. She wrote an autobiography, *Fifteen-Thirty*, and a novel.

In her prime she and her husband traveled extensively through the Orient and Europe, playing exhibitions and writing for American newspapers on fashion trends in the salons of Paris, a Rembrandt exhibition in Amsterdam, horse racing, openings of dressmaking houses, and automobile and flower shows. She once wrote, "One notes that tennis championships are not all-important." Another time she said, "Tennis is a diversion, not a career." In fact, she almost did not bother to go to the 1929 championships at Wimbledon. "When I decided to make the trip to Wimbledon, it was two o'clock in the afternoon and I managed to catch the eight o'clock train that evening . . . The visa had to be left until I reached New York when I also picked up my rackets."

Perhaps her finest accomplishment was that she raised the quality of women's tennis to the point where its coverage in the press was equal to the men's. Today Helen Wills Moody lives in retirement in California.

The Pioneers

Glenna Collett Vare

"The Wonder Woman of American Golf"
June 20, 1903–
New Haven, Connecticut

Glenna Collett was the first great American woman golfer. Before she set the competitive tone, women's golf was a game played by a privileged few with no spectator appeal. She made golf respectable and popular.

Collett was a late starter on the links, although always a fine natural athlete who swam and dove well and even played baseball on her brother's team. But one summer day in 1918, when Glenna was 15, her father brought her to see Alexa Stirling, the reigning golf queen, play an exhibition in Rhode Island. Little did she realize that she would play against Stirling for the championship of the United States within a few years.

Buoyed by her father's encouragement, Collett practiced golf seriously. She received lessons from Alex Smith, the teaching professional at the Shennecossett Club in New London, Connecticut, and a two-time winner of the United States Open, and within four years was good enough to win the United States Amateur Championship.

Golf competition was still in its infancy in Glenna Collett's day. There were no tour events in which professionals competed weekly. People played for club, sectional, and, if they were good enough, national championships. Travel abroad was limited; it took more than a week to cross the Atlantic to enter a European event. Championships were decided by match play in which 128 contestants qualified in a medal round and then paired off in single elimination matches until a champion emerged undefeated from the pack. Golf clubs had wooden shafts and golf balls were dead when compared with today's rockets. The greens were not manicured as neatly as today, nor were the fairways the consistently-cut grass that current professionals take for granted.

Collett's first major victory occurred in Philadelphia in 1921 when the 18-year-old fledgling defeated Britain's Cecil Leitch in the finals to take the Berthellyn Cup. Leich won the British Ladies Championship three times. Her first United States Ladies Championship came in 1922, her second in 1925. In between she won 59 of the 60 matches during the 1924 season. Many fine women golfers emerged during the post–World War era, free to play in comfortable clothing and without social stigma. Mary Kimball Browne, who was also a great tennis player, was a star. Edith Cummings, Dorothy Campbell Hurd, and Helen Stetson were national champions. But Collett rose above them

Glenna Collett, America's premier woman golfer of the twenties and thirties (photo courtesy Golf Housé).

with her third national title in 1928. In convincing style she came through the match-play elimination rounds to meet Virginia Van Wie in the 36-hole final match. Collett's first nine took 36 strokes, an amazing score for the way golf was then played. New York Times correspondent, James Richardson enthusiastically wrote, "It was certainly the finest golf that has ever been seen in the final round of any women's championship in this country." Collett played the back nine in 41 to set a women's record at 77 for the Hot Springs, Virginia course. Poor Van Wie, who could not get her game together, found herself down ten holes after the first eighteen holes. Collett was up 13 holes with 12 to go, after six holes of the second round. The 13–12 margin was the largest recorded in women's national play, surpassing Collett's 9–8 victory over Alexa Stirling in 1925. Van Wie later won the national women's crown for three consecutive years from 1932 through 1934.

Collett clearly established herself as the finest American woman golfer of her era with repeat victories in 1929 and 1930, her fourth and fifth titles.

Glenna had moderate success competing in foreign national championships. She won the Canadian Ladies Open in 1923 and 1924 and the French Ladies Open in 1925. She competed in the British national championship four times but never won, although she advanced to the finals in 1929 and 1930, only to be defeated by England's Joyce Wethered and Diana Fishwick, respectively.

Glenna Collett was runner-up for the United States title in 1931 and 1932. She married Edward H. Vare in 1931 and subsequently found little time for competitive golf. The Vares were married for 44 years until Edward's death in 1975. But Glenna Collett Vare, a 32-year-old mother of two and 13 years removed from her first championship, won her final championship against Patty Berg, the 17-year-old freckled-faced kid and darling of the hometown Minneapolis fans. Vare played the front nine at Interlachen Country Club in 40 to go two up on young Miss Berg. She completed the round in 79, one over women's par, and four holes up on Berg. But Berg was a champion in the making and rallied in the afternoon, playing her more experienced opponent evenly through nine holes. They split the tenth, eleventh, and twelfth, but Berg won the next two holes putting the pressure on Vare, who's lead was down to two holes. They halved the fifteenth, and Vare birdied the sixteenth to win the match, 3–2. It was her sixth, and last, national championship.

The era that Glenna Collett dominated was the first in which more than a few women competed at the national level in golf. When she started, a score in the mid–80s won a tournament; championships were won with ten fewer strokes at the end of her career. Collett had a complete game except for one flaw. She was only a so-so putter until late in her career, although she became deadly on the greens as her game matured. Inevitably, because their careers coincided, she was known as the "Bobby Jones of Women's Golf." Coincidentally, Jones, who was a good friend of Collett's, retired from competition to pursue his law career the day she won her third consecutive United States title in 1930. Bobby Jones said of Collett that "her accuracy with the spoon and brassie [fairway woods] is the most important part of her well-rounded game. It is her way of absorbing the disadvantage of length some women suffer against the best males, but she does it with little disadvantage."

Glenna drove 200 yards off the tee regularly and with exceptional accuracy. That was only a few yards shorter than the best men players of that era could manage. Some witnesses say that she occasionally hit the ball 300 yards when conditions were right. But steadiness was the feature of her game; she simply turned in a lower score than her opponents because she seldom made mistakes. She earned the nickname "The Wonder Woman of American Golf." An Associated Press release, describing her victory over Virginia Van Wie in the 1930 United States Championship, says: "As calmly as though out for a couple of practice rounds, the defending champion of the last two years pitted her mastery of the woods and irons against the challenge of the younger rival. Oblivious to everything, including frequent applause from several thousand spectators, Miss Collett set a steady pace that produced the best golf of the tournament.'"

She played on, and captained, the United States Curtis Cup team in international play in 1934, 1936, and 1948. In 1950 she was the team's non-playing captain. Her books, *Golf for Young Players* and *Ladies in the Rough*, were published in 1926 and 1928, respectively. In 1952, Glenna Collett Vare donated the Vare Trophy, to be awarded to the player on the Ladies Professional Golf Association (LPGA) tour with the lowest annual per-round score. It was a most appropriate gift from the person who brought consistent low scoring to women's golf.

In 1981, at the age of 78, she was still playing to an 11 handicap and played into her 80s.

Always popular with the press and galleries, she was intelligent, witty and pretty—the sort of wholesome charmer popular with sports fans of that day. Her name will live on in golf as a wonderful woman and champion.

Charlotte Dod

"The Little Wonder"
September 24, 1871–October 10, 1962
Great Britain

Charlotte "Lottie Dod" was the first superstar of women's sports. Only Babe Didrikson has surpassed her versatility as a female athlete.

Lottie Dod won the Wimbledon Tennis championship five times: 1887, 1888, 1891, 1892, and 1893. Five Wimbledon titles alone normally qualifies an athlete as an all-time great, but Dod was also an outstanding skater, tobogganner, and a "Field Hockey International" for Great Britain in 1899. She took the British Ladies Golf title in 1904 and an Olympic silver medal for archery in 1908.

Charlotte Dod grew up in Britain during the Victorian Age. Queen Victoria, for whom the era was named, ruled Britain from 1837 until 1901. Although she herself was a vigorous and powerful woman, the monarch expected other women to be docile homebodies who did not engage in physical activities. Women were to be genteel, participating in sports only as a casual pastime. Croquet was the most popular sport for men and women in both the United States and Great Britain.

The annual tennis tournament at Wimbledon for the British championship provided women with their first opportunity to compete in an energetic sport. In 1884 Maud Watson defeated L. Watson for the first Ladies All-English title. Three years later, Charlotte Dod, nicknamed "The Little Wonder," took over the tournament and dominated it for nearly seven years.

The record book shows that Lottie defeated B. James 6–1, 6–1 in the quarterfinals, and C. J. Cole, 6–2, 6–3, in the semis. She outclassed defending champion, Blanche Bingley, 6–2, 6–0 in the finals.

Lottie had a reputation as a "giant killer" even earlier. When she was 14 years old she defeated Maud Watson at a match at Bath breaking a 55-match consecutive winning streak that had begun in 1881.

Charlotte had an advantage when she won the British title in 1887. She was a fifteen-year-old schoolgirl and was allowed to play in her school uniform, which featured a calf-length skirt. Women normally played tennis in ground-length skirts that covered several petticoats and a binding corset several inches smaller than the lady's waist. Wire stays often dug into the flesh of players as they strained to return well-positioned shots. As late as 1905, Dod wrote, "Hearty indeed would be the thanks of puzzled lady players to the individual who invented an easy and pretty costume." Later championships had to be waged encumbered like her opponents, yet her victory in 1887, when she was 15 years and ten months old, still stands as the youngest age for a Wimbledon champion.

The only set she ever lost at Wimbledon was to Blanche Bingley Hilliard in 1893, but she still won the final, 6–8, 6–1, 6–4. Hilliard was also a five-time Wimbledon singles champion. Dod won the doubles championship at Wimbledon in 1886 through 1888; the mixed doubles in 1889 and 1892, and the Irish national singles and mixed doubles titles in 1887.

One of her secrets was that she was the first woman tennis player to study the style of the men. She introduced the smash to ladies' play and won consistently because she was more aggressive than her opponents. She even played exhibitions against the reigning Wimbledon men's champion, William Renshaw.

Tennis was no longer a challenge after the 1893 victory, and in 1894, at the age of 21, she retired from the game to devote more time to golf, archery, and field hockey. She was the first woman to complete the Cresta bobsled run at St. Moritz and was an excellent ice skater. She later became an international judge in figure skating competition.

Consider what women's sports were like in the nineteenth century. Croquet, archery, tennis, and golf were considered appropriate sports for women, as long as the players participated in the mandated bulky clothing. Sports were accepted in which women seldom were subjected to that demeaning activity — perspiring. Sports in general were usually reserved for the rich; it was a way in which the well-to-do could conspicuously display their leisure time. Sports also provided an opportunity for men and women to meet each other socially in a time of restricted contact. Croquet was ideal. Both men and women participated, and nobody sweat.

Dod died in 1960 at age 89, having witnessed two world wars, the extension of the voting franchise to women and women's full participation in international and Olympic competition. In 1986, 99 years after her first Wimbledon title, Lottie Dod was inducted into the International Women's Hall of Fame.

Amelia Mary Earhart

"Lady Lindy"
July 24, 1897–July 2, 1937
Atchison, Kansas

Amelia Earhart, a great athlete? Amelia Earhart is not only the famous aviatrix but a charter member of the Women's International Sports Foundation Hall of Fame. In the early days of aviation pilots were indeed athletes.

The air age began in Kitty Hawk, North Carolina, on December 17, 1903, when Orville Wright flew the plane he and his brother Wilber built in a 12-second flight that covered 120 feet. Flying's first fatality occurred in 1908, and two years later, Baroness Raymonde de la Roche of France became the first woman to earn a pilot's license. During World War I, aircraft served a relatively minor role in reconnaissance, although much has been written about the theatrical aerial dogfights that occasionally took place.

By 1918 airplanes were ferrying mail across the United States and the Atlantic was crossed non-stop by a team of pilots in 1919. But today it is difficult to grasp the excitement and joy generated when Charles Augustus Lindbergh landed "The Spirit of St. Louis" at Le Bourget Field near Paris on May 21, 1927, ending the first solo, non-stop, transatlantic flight. Americans sought a hero and the good-looking, intelligent, and brave Lindbergh was perfect for the role.

Today passengers board the Concorde at New York's Kennedy International Airport and less than four hours later pick up their luggage in Paris or London. Lindbergh flew for 33 hours and 39 minutes with poor weather information and virtually no navigational aids, in a cockpit that reeked of gasoline fumes. It was a manly endeavor, certainly no task for a woman. Scores of people who attempted the feat both before and after Lindbergh were lost at sea. Earhart became a national heroine, almost as well known as Lindbergh, when she accomplished a series of highly-publicized flying achievements.

Amelia was born in Atchison, Kansas, three years before the turn of the century, to Edwin and Amy Otis Earhart. Edwin was brilliant. He was graduated from Thiel College, Greenville, Pennsylvania, at age 18, but then lived an unsuccessful life fighting alcoholism. Amy Otis's family was from the finest social circle in Kansas.

Amelia grew up knowing that she wanted to do something important, but she was not sure what. Interested in learning and a fine student, she dropped

Amelia Earhart in 1934 (photo courtesy the Wichita *Eagle*).

out of school three times and never finished her college work at Columbia University. She was a nurse at a Toronto convalescent hospital, and at one time considered a career in medicine. Later she was a social worker. But in 1921, when she was 24, Amelia learned to fly and was consumed by the experience. The airplane became her life and obsessive love.

During these pioneering days, Amelia became one of approximately a score of women who held a pilot's license. Although she set an unofficial women's altitude record at 14,000 feet in 1922, she was far from being the finest woman pilot in the world in those early days. She was a little reckless and escaped serious injury in more than one crack-up.

Earhart became famous because she was in the right place at the right time and projected the right image. After Lindbergh's flight in 1927, people began to wonder who would be the first woman to fly the Atlantic. A group headed by George Putnam, the publisher from G. P. Putnam's Sons, and Admiral Richard Byrd, the explorer, organized an expedition to accomplish this feat. They selected Earhart because she could fly, was "the right kind of person," and greatly resembled Charles Lindbergh. She crossed the Atlantic on June 18, 1928, as a passenger in a plane piloted by one man and navigated by another. Because Putnam handled the publicity so well, Amelia Earhart became the most famous woman in the world, and the two men, Wilmer Stultz and Louis Gordon, are virtually unknown to history.

Although she received a ticker-tape parade in New York and was acclaimed throughout the world, she knew that she contributed little to the flight's success. She was determined to make it on her own as a pilot. Within a few years she was acknowledged to be among the best and bravest pilots of all time.

Amelia supported herself by lecturing on the celebrity circuit and saved enough money to buy her own airplane. Later in 1928 she became the first woman to solo, round-trip, across the continental United States. During the flight she stopped at many towns for personal appearances and received a tumultuous reception at each. In 1930, she set a women's speed record of 181 miles per hour. In 1931 she married her publicist, George Putnam, in what she termed "a marriage of convenience." She pursued her career; Putnam managed and partially financed it, while continuing to pursue his many interests.

In May of 1932 Amelia Earhart "earned her wings" to her own satisfaction when she became the first woman, and only the second person to fly the Atlantic solo and non-stop. She earned the title, "the best known woman in America."

Amelia received many prestigious awards. President Herbert Hoover presented her with the Gold Medal of the National Geographic Society. Congress awarded her the Distinguished Flying Cross, and France presented her the Cross of Knight of the Legion of Honor. Eleanor Roosevelt was her personal friend. She continued to lecture and write, but flying was in her blood.

In 1935, Earhart became the first person to fly solo from Hawaii to California. She then flew non-stop from Mexico City to Newark, New Jersey. In 1936, she began planning a round-the-world trip in a plane provided by Purdue University. It would be her last venture.

The famous flight began in Miami, Florida. "I have the feeling there is just one more flight in my system" Amelia, who was nearing 40, said to a friend. "This trip around the world is it." She planned to settle down for keeps. With her experienced navigator, Fred Noonan, she first flew southeast, stopping at Puerto Rico, Venezuela, Dutch Guiana, and Brazil. From there came the hop across the Atlantic to French West Africa. She crossed Africa with stops at Chad, the Sudan, and Ethiopia. At this point she was halfway around the world. Then it was on to Karachi, Calcutta, Rangoon, Singapore, Java, Darwin, Australia, and Lae, New Guinea. She had travelled more than 20,000 miles in approximately three weeks. But the vast Pacific lay ahead.

Amelia's next stop was scheduled to be at Howland Island, a tiny speck in the middle of a vast ocean where the United States maintained a small naval base. She never reached it. The base lost radio contact with her when she was apparently within a few miles of the island. Despite the largest air and sea search ever conducted, no trace has ever been found of Earhart and Noonan.

The legend of Amelia Earhart has been growing since, fueled by mystery and speculation. A movie produced during World War II, *Flight to Freedom*, told the story of a woman pilot who became deliberately lost at sea in the Pacific to provide the United States with an excuse to investigate what the Japanese were doing in the area; people concluded that it was based on the life of Amelia Earhart. Doris Rich, who wrote an authoritative biography on Earhart in 1989 concluded simply: "She lost her way on a flight from Lae, New Guinea to Howland Island and died somewhere in the Pacific."

Gertrude Ederle

"Trudy"
October 23, 1906–
New York, New York

It was a few minutes after seven on a bright August morning. Gertrude Ederle paused for a moment on the beach at Cap Gris-Nez, France, to think about the task ahead of her. She wore a one-piece bathing suit, goggles, and was greased from head-to-toe with an insulating concoction of olive oil, Vaseline, lard, and lanolin. She slowly waded into the water, which soon engulfed her broad-shouldered, five-feet, five-inch, 135-pound frame. Ederle then began the methodical stroking that 15 hours later would make her the most celebrated woman in the world. The English Channel, with all its treacherous tides, currents, and numbing cold, was about to be conquered.

Gertrude Ederle became America's first female superstar swimmer on August 6, 1926, when she successfully crossed the English Channel. At the time, it may have been the greatest single athletic endeavor of the century. The front-page headline of the August 7 *New York Times* proclaimed:

GERTRUDE EDERLE SWIMS THE CHANNEL
IN RECORD TIME OF 14 HOURS 31 MINUTES
AMERICAN IS FIRST WOMAN TO CROSS

Ederle was the first woman and only the sixth person to swim the Channel. Her time was one hour and 52 minutes faster than the best time of the five men who preceded her.

Paul Gallico, the flamboyant sports writer of the "roaring twenties," called the swim, "the greatest recorded athletic feat by a woman in the history of the world." Annette Kellerman, a swimming great who had made the attempt before Ederle and failed, concluded that swimming the English Channel was "totally beyond the limits of a woman's strength and endurance."

Trudy Ederle came from a German section on New York's west side, the same part of town that produced another well-known German-American, her contemporary, Lou Gehrig. Her father was a butcher and delicatessen owner, her mother a housewife. They did well enough to have a summer cottage in Highlands, New Jersey, less than 20 miles from mid-town Manhattan. Young Trudy first discovered her natural swimming ability romping in the waves on hot summer days at the New Jersey shore.

Gertrude learned to dog paddle at nine; an age when Mark Spitz was winning national age-group titles. She did not learn to swim properly until she was 15 and began training at the Women's Swimming Association of New York. Within three years she was good enough to win Olympic bronze medals in the 100- and 400-meter freestyle, and a gold medal in the 400-meter freestyle relay at the 1924 Games. Between 1921 and 1925, Gertrude held 29 amateur and world records at events from 50 yards to one-half mile. One day in 1922 she broke seven world records at Brooklyn's Brighton Beach while competing in a 500-meter swim. But these were only warm-ups toward one goal—to swim the English Channel. To do it, she became a professional in 1925.

Ederle's first channel attempt in 1925 failed when she was within six and one-half miles of the British shore. She did not want to quit, but her trainer feared she was swallowing too much salt water and deliberately touched her,

Gertrude Ederle being greased before her successful channel swim (photo courtesy International Swimming Hall of Fame).

causing a disqualification. She was back again in the summer of 1926, and this time the 20-year-old would not be denied.

Gertrude Ederle entered the chilly channel waters at Cape Gris-Nez at 7:09 A.M. on August 6, and reached Kingsdorn, near Dover, at 9:40 P.M. That evening the British beach was alive with bonfires that illuminated the shores to guide the American to her destination. The jubilant reception as she came out of the water was only the first of many for the new celebrity. She was feted in the major cities of Europe before her triumphal return to New York, where 2 million people greeted her in one of the city's most famous ticker-tape parades.

A model of clean living, she never smoked, drank, nor caroused and was liked and admired by everyone who knew her. W. O. McGeehan described her as having "the simplicity of Shaw's St. Joan and the physique of a male giant." President Calvin Coolidge called her "America's best girl."

But after her spectacular success, Ederle has lived the rest of her life in relative obscurity, with an unfair amount of bad luck. Her professional career was mismanaged, and although she briefly made $2000 per week on the vaudeville circuit giving swimming exhibitions and answering questions, she ultimately made little money from her success. The Channel swim permanently impaired her hearing, and she became totally deaf by 1933. During the 1930s she suffered a nervous breakdown. After that, a back injury, resulting from falling down a flight of stairs, forced her to wear a cast for four and one-half years. She was a fashion designer and spent much of her time teaching deaf children to swim. She swam in Billy Rose's Aquacade during the 1939 New York World's Fair and during World War II repaired aircraft parts. Ederle lived most of her life quietly in a small house which she shared with two friends in Flushing, New York. Her last public appearance was in 1976 on the fiftieth anniversary of her historic swim. She said then, "If God called me tomorrow, I'd go willingly. I've had a full life, a beautiful life." At this writing she is alive and in her 80s.

Ederle was the first person to demonstrate that it was possible for a woman to compete with men in some sports, and to share in the acclaim showered on sports heroes. Ironically, on the day of her channel swim, an editorial in the London *Daily News* pontificated: "Even the most uncompromising champion of the rights and capacities of women must admit that in contests of physical skill, speed, and endurance, they must remain the weaker sex."

In her later years, Trudy once was quoted as saying, "I'm comfortable . . . I saved money . . . I've never been helped . . . it didn't matter if they've forgotten me. I haven't forgotten them. It was worth it."

Some of us haven't forgotten.

Eleanor Holm

"In the limelight"
December 6, 1913–
Brooklyn, New York

Eleanor Holm succeeded Gertrude Ederle as the best-known swimmer in the world, but unlike the proper Ederle, Holm was a hell-raiser. Also a New Yorker, born and raised in Brooklyn, her father was a fire captain. Eleanor created a few "three-alarmers" in her heyday.

Eleanor Holm, circa 1932 (photo courtesy International Swimming Hall of Fame).

Holm was a specialist, a backstroker; probably the finest ever. As a 14-year-old, she finished fifth in the 100-meter backstroke at the 1928 Olympics at Amsterdam. By 1932, she was the best in the world in the event, winning the Olympic gold medal and setting a world record during a preliminary heat. Her time was nearly three seconds faster than the standard established in 1928. In the period between 1929 and 1932 Eleanor established a new world record for the backstroke at every recorded distance.

A beautiful young woman, as a 16-year-old she danced as a Ziegfeld showgirl. After her triumph in the 1932 Olympics, she signed a $500-per-week contract with Warner Brothers. This was the time of the Great Depression and $500 represented quite a sum of money. Eleanor soon had a falling out with Warner Brothers. They wanted her to perform as a swimmer in the movies, but if she did, she would be declared a professional and be ineligible for future swimming competition. When the offer became $750 to swim, or nothing, she opted for nothing.

In 1933 she married band leader and fellow Brooklynite, Art Jarrett, in Beverly Hills, became a nightclub singer, and for the next three years lived the Hollywood lifestyle of a big band singer. When the band travelled, she worked at night and during the day trained at whatever pool was available. Eleanor once said, "I train on champagne and cigarettes," but she never lost her competitive skills. By the time the 1936 United States Olympic swimming team was selected, she had established new world records for the backstroke at 100 meters and 200 meters, and had been undefeated in competition for seven years. She joined her Olympic teammates aboard the SS *Manhattan* for the trip to Berlin as the favorite to defend her backstroke title.

It was the voyage which sank a swimmer. The United States Olympic Committee, led by Avery Brundage, banned her from the games for misbehavior aboard ship. Jarrett was used to being the life of the party and resented the third-class accommodations afforded the athletes, particularly when the press and Olympic officials went first-class. No one, especially the offender, ever denied that she partied. When accused of "acute alcoholism" and shooting craps, her defense was that she won "a couple of hundred dollars" on the voyage.

In 1936, the Olympic Committee, guided by Brundage, had produced a handbook with a set of regulations that team members were expected to adhere to. One rule read: "It is understood of course that all members of the American team refrain from smoking and the use of intoxicating drinks and other forms of dissipation in training."

Jarrett did party until well into the morning with members of the press, including Charles MacArthur, the husband of Helen Hayes. She thoroughly violated the rule.

Brundage had already tried to take Eleanor's amateur status away in 1934 and declared that the Olympic Committee "considered all grounds for leniency and found none."

Eleanor was banned from all future Olympic, as well as amateur, competition in the United States and Europe. Despite a petition signed by 200 teammates, the ban stuck, but it did not even slow her down. The party continued in Berlin where she was an instant celebrity. Jarrett later said, "I enjoyed the parties, the Heil Hitlers, the uniforms, the flags. . . . Göring was fun. He gave me a sterling silver swastika. I had a mold made of it, and I put a diamond Star of David in the middle."

Eleanor's amateur swimming career was through, but she remained in the limelight for quite some time. In 1937, she was making $2500 per week on the vaudeville circuit and also starred in a Tarzan movie, "Tarzan's Revenge." She divorced Art Jarrett in 1938, and in 1939 married show business impresario, Billy Rose, starring in his 1939 Aquacade at the New York World's Fair. With World War II approaching, it was proposed that the 1940 Olympics be held in New York in conjunction with the World's Fair, where the banned Eleanor Rose was a key attraction. The 1940 games were never conducted.

Her 1954 divorce from Rose was a tabloid item for months. She later became an interior decorator, and lives in retirement in Florida. She was selected to the International Swimming Hall of Fame in 1966 and was one of the first six to be ushered into the International Women's Hall of Fame in 1980. Interviewed by the New York Times in 1984 about how fit she was, the 71-year-old said, "I don't swim anymore. I just play tennis. But I still have my 1932 Olympic bathing suit." Actually, she still filled it out quite well and, one suspects, could still swim as effortlessly as she did when she was the best in the world.

Suzanne Rachel Flore Lenglen
"The Greatest of Them All"
March 24, 1900–July 4, 1938
Compiegne, France

Suzanne Lenglen single-handedly established women's tennis as a full-fledged sport through her sheer skill and personality. She was "box office."

Suzanne Lenglen in a 1924 match at Cannes, France (photo courtesy Wide World Photos).

Born in Compiegne, in the south of France, her parents were moderately well off and arranged for professional tennis lessons for Suzanne when it was apparent that she was a gifted player. As a 14-year-old she won the women's singles and doubles at the 1914 World Hard Court championships in Paris, but World War I put her career on hold for five years. Play for the All-England championships at Wimbledon resumed in 1919, and Lenglen's performance there permanently changed women's tennis.

44 Suzanne Rachel Flore Lenglen

Dorothea Lambert Chambers had won the Wimbledon crown six times, including 1914, and since competition was suspended from 1915 through 1918 she was the defending titleist. At that time the reigning champion did not participate in the preliminary rounds and only played when the best challenger emerged from the competition. Lenglen breezed through the contenders to challenge the 41-year-old tennis master for the title.

Lenglen won the first set, 10–8, but Chambers came back to win the next set, 6–4. In the grueling finale, Lenglen outlasted her veteran opponent, 9–7, to become the new "Queen of Tennis," a title she did not relinquish until she became a professional in 1926.

During her Wimbledon appearance, Miss Lenglen wore a one-piece dress that bared her arms and only came to her mid-calves, showing her stockinged legs. The gallery was aghast at such brazenness, but in subsequent years she established the standards for comfortable tennis attire. The headband she popularized became known as the Lenglen Bandeaux and was the rage of fashion salons everywhere. Helen Jacobs described her as "not good looking, but with tremendous personality and charm." Cartoonists of the time often exaggerated her large, hooked nose, large mouth, and heavily rouged cheeks. But her grace in movement was second to no one; she was a ballerina on the court.

At home on French courts Lenglen was literally unbeatable, winning the six French Championships she entered. She won the 1926 title while only losing four games. Her Wimbledon performances are legendary:

Year	Women's Singles	Women's Doubles	Mixed Doubles
1919	won	won	won
1920	won	won	
1921	won	won	
1922*	won	won	won
1923	won	won	
1924	withdrew because of illness		
1925	won	won	won
1926	withdrew	lost	

*Beginning in 1922, the defending champion was required to play in the preliminary rounds.

In singles play, she won each of her thirty-two matches, played a total of sixty-six sets and lost only two. Twenty-nine times she shut out her opponents, 6–0. Tennis was an Olympic sport in 1920, and Lenglen won both the singles and mixed-doubles gold medals.

As Suzanne Lenglen lost only one recorded match from her first appearance at Wimbledon in 1919 until the end of her amateur career in 1926. In 1921, in a rare appearance at the United States National Championships, she bowed out of a match with Molla Mallory of the United States after losing the first set and falling behind in the second. The American press branded her a quitter, but the real reason for withdrawing related to a long history of serious physical problems.

Lenglen was never well. Her default to Mallory was caused by whooping cough. As a child, she was afflicted with frequent asthma attacks. Her parents encouraged tennis to improve her health, and that incredible streak at Wimbledon of women's singles and doubles titles was interrupted in 1924 when an attack of jaundice forced her retirement from play. Retiring from amateur competition to tour the United States as a professional, the player's success on tour was marred when she frequently was required to withdraw from appearances because of ill health. She died at the tragically-young age of thirty-nine in 1938.

The most publicized match of Lenglen's career was against the rising American star, Helen Wills. The hype for the match dominated sports-page headlines throughout the world for weeks. The match was held in Cannes, France, in February 1926. The more experienced Lenglen defeated her nineteen-year-old opponent, 6–3, 8–6. Miss Wills, who became an all-time great, later said of Suzanne, "She had more generalship on the court than I did . . . I had more power and endurance." They never played each other again as Lenglen became a professional later that year.

Suzanne Lenglen's last appearance at Wimbledon was a debacle. Because of a scheduling mix-up, she was an hour late arriving for her singles match because she thought that she was reporting for a doubles match scheduled for later in the day. Worse, she had kept the royal family, who had come to see the great Frenchwoman play, waiting idly in the royal box. She was thoroughly chastised and subsequently lost her doubles match. Thoroughly upset by the affair, she withdrew from the tournament, never to play amateur tennis again. The French government apologized to the Queen.

There is little doubt that Lenglen was a supreme prima donna, "a genius on the courts with all the temperament of a great artiste." When it was cold she took the court in a full-length fur coat which she dramatically removed when it was time to warm up. When things went against her, she was known to stomp her feet and shed tears until conditions met her satisfaction. One authority referred to her as "the most colorful, temperamental and tempestuous of all feminine athletes."

Suzanne toured the States in late 1926 and early 1927, working with noted entrepreneur, C. C. (facetiously called "cash and carry") Pyle. Lenglen drew 13,000 to New York's Madison Square Garden for the tour's kickoff, but subsequent events were not well planned and the overall results of the tour were, at best, mixed. Suzanne returned to France in 1927 to the life of celebrity and author. Some still say that she was the best who ever played the game.

Trent Frayne, in his book, *Famous Women Tennis Players*, succinctly states, "No one changed the face of women's tennis the way Suzanne Lenglen did, not even Billy Jean King who came along four decades later leading a revolution." And Elizabeth Ryan, who played her frequently and who won nineteen Wimbledon championships, says, "Sure, she was a poser, a ham in the theatrical sense . . . but she was the greatest woman player of them all. Never doubt that."

Annie Oakley

Born Phoebe June Moses
"Doin' what comes naturally"
August 13, 1860–November 3, 1926
Patterson Township, Darke County, Ohio

Annie Oakley came out of the rough-and-tumble frontier during the well-chronicled period that followed the United States Civil War. She competed with men in rifle marksmanship, the most popular, macho sport in the West. She was as good as there was.

Phoebe June Moses was the fifth of Jacob and Susan Moses's eight children. The Moseses were Quakers, who moved to Ohio, near Cincinnati, from western Pennsylvania several years before Annie was born. Jacob Moses died from exposure in a blizzard in March of 1864 when Phoebe was four. The family was split up when her mother worked as a district nurse and could not care for all of them. After staying with her mother until she was nine the girl was sent to an orphanage. After a year there she was dispatched to a farm family, forced to work 12 hours a day and physically abused. At 12, she was old enough and wise enough to run away and eventually was reunited with her mother who had remarried. About that time Phoebe found one of her father's old rifles and began hunting to help support the family. The story is told that she brought so many rabbits and quail to the market in Cincinnati that she paid off the mortgage on the family house for her mother and stepfather. Perhaps that is an exaggeration, but it is easy to believe the story that every bird she brought to market had been shot cleanly through the head, based on her later record.

The girl who became Annie Oakley displayed three skills that all great athletes possess: eye-hand coordination, timing, and courage. When she was 16 she visited her sister in Cincinnati, and a few people who knew her ability suggested a contest with Frank Butler, a professional marksman and travelling vaudevillian. Butler lost by one point, although some suggest Frank did not try his best, for the 16-year-old girl had caught the eye of the 26-year-old sharpshooter. It is clear that Annie was a much better shot than Frank in later years. Although he lost the contest, Frank won Phoebe, and they were married on June 22, 1876, and remained married until Annie's death 50 years later. Frank died three weeks later.

Annie Oakley was an outstanding competitive marksperson who would have been an Olympic champion in a later era. In 1887 she ran off 100 consecutive hits in trap shooting, a feat she repeated many times. Her last 100-for-100 occurred in 1922 when she was 62; she consistently hit 97 out of 100 when she was 65.

Professional trapshooting contests were a favorite in the towns along the Ohio River. Usually the winner took all the prize money. Phoebe Butler won $5000 one year in these contests, the equivalent of hundreds of thousands of dollars today. But since there was no professional sports competition in the late 1800s, she earned her living in show business, as did many other athletes. Frank Butler became her partner, manager, and assistant. They were a great team, and he managed her career well. Soon after they were married, Butler and Oakley began touring the Midwest vaudeville circuit. Annie adopted her last name, Oakley, from a town in Ohio and learned how to perform in public from Frank. Butler also taught his unschooled wife to read and write and how to display her winning disposition to an audience. After a few years they became headliners in their business.

As Butler got older, he took a lesser role in the act and Annie Oakley became the star. They worked in the Sells Brothers Circus, and, with Frank doing the negotiations, Annie became the feature attraction of Buffalo Bill's Wild West Show in 1885. Annie performed with the show, which was the first rodeo, for 16 years. Even the great Sioux chief Sitting Bull took second billing to Annie's trick shot act.

Annie opened her act with a display of marksmanship on foot, followed by a horseback exhibition. On foot she shot glass balls which had been tossed in the air, using both a rifle and shotgun. Her most difficult trick was to lie on her back while Frank Butler threw six glass balls in the air. Three double-barreled shotguns would discharge, breaking all six balls before they hit the ground. She then would hit a cigarette held between Frank's lips with a rifle and nail a dime

Annie Oakley as she looked when she traveled with Buffalo Bill Cody's Wild West Show (photo courtesy American Trapshooting Hall of Fame).

tossed in the air ninety feet away. Her trademark was precision shooting using playing cards. At thirty paces she would split a playing card held parallel to the ground. She would then have someone toss a card in the air and would fire several shots through it. For decades a pass for free admission to an event was called an "Annie Oakley" because the holes punched through it were reminiscent of Oakley's bullet-punctured cards.

Annie Oakley became one of the most famous women in the world when she toured the United States and Europe with the Buffalo Bill Circus. She performed for the Kaiser in Germany and was presented to Queen Victoria in England. Offstage Annie Oakley was soft-spoken, gentle, and likeable. Standing under five feet tall and weighing about 98 pounds, she was a particular favorite with the rugged circus people. Sitting Bull gave her the Sioux name, "My Daughter, Little Sure Shot." Bible reading was her favorite pastime, and she remained true to her pious Quaker background. She also meticulously kept track of every penny she and Frank earned.

Annie was severely injured in a train wreck in Virginia in 1901 and never performed in the rodeo after that. She earned a living playing western heroines on the stage and giving shooting lessons. Her marksmanship exhibitions were a favorite of the World War I doughboys.

Annie had a second serious mishap, an automobile accident in 1922 in Florida, from which she never fully recovered. She returned to Ohio shortly before her death at the age of 66 in 1926.

Many accounts of her life have been written but the highly romanticized "Annie Get Your Gun" by Herbert and Dorothy Fields, to which Irving Berlin wrote the lyrics and music, will last for generations. One of Berlin's songs from the show, "Doin' What Comes Naturally," sums up Annie Oakley well. She was a natural athlete and a naturally-fine person—someone to admire.

Eleonora Randolph Sears

"Eleo"
September 28, 1881–March 26, 1968
Boston, Massachusetts

Irving Berlin also wrote the song "Anything You Can Do I Can Do Better" for the musical about Annie Oakley, "Annie Get Your Gun," but the words are probably more appropriate for Eleonora Sears. She did everything well.

Eleonora Sears, a great all-around athlete. Notice her rolled up sleeves which were considered a shocking display in her day (photo courtesy International Tennis Hall of Fame and Tennis Museum at the Newport Casino, Newport, RI).

Eleonora was born in the latter part of the nineteenth century, so was limited in sports opportunities as has been noted. But Eleo had advantages most people do not enjoy. She came from well-bred, well-monied, Boston socialites. Her father, Frederick Richard Sears, descendent of early New England settlers and a successful real estate and shipping tycoon, provided the money. Her mother, Eleonora Randolph Coolidge Sears, provided the lineage. Eleo's grandfather, Thomas Jefferson Coolidge, was minister to France in 1892 and 1893. Thomas Jefferson was her great, great-granfather.

Eleo grew up in luxury and was educated by private tutors. She loved the outdoors and learned to swim, play tennis and golf, and ride horses at an early age. She lived the life of the very rich: winters on Boston's Beacon Hill, summers twenty miles to the west at the family estate at Pride's Crossing. In her early twenties, Eleo became "the belle of the ball" at Newport, Rhode Island's, social swirl. Society's elite summered at the famous Newport "cottages," among the finest mansions in the country. During the day they played tennis at the Casino on Bellvue Drive, the current site of the Tennis Hall of Fame. In the evenings they danced at the gala balls where the rich rubbed elbows with the titled. Eleo starred both day and night.

Sears had her first sports success at the Newport Casino when she quickly became the finest woman playing tennis there. She played more aggressively than her competitors and soon her friends encouraged her to compete in the open women's tournaments. In 1911, when she was thirty, she teamed with Hazel Hotchkiss Wightman, after whom the Wightman Cup was later named, to win the United States women's doubles championship. From 1911 through 1917 she was one of the top players in the country, winning the doubles title again with Hotchkiss in 1915 and successfully defending it in 1916 and 1917 with partner Molla Bjurstedt Mallory. She also won the mixed doubles in 1916 with Willie Davis. Eleo was twice a finalist in the national singles competition. But Eleonora's tennis game raised eyebrows because of her habit of rolling up her sleeves when she played, baring her arms. She got away with it because of who she was. Eleo loved to raise eyebrows.

Sears was the finest horsewoman in the United States for decades. She said that she rode four hours a day during most of her adult life. She was already an expert rider when she was a child and frequently participated in the hunt with the men. She was visiting in Buringame, California, one day in 1912 and spent a few moments resting from riding to watch a practice men's polo game. Eleonora spontaneously rode onto the field to see if she could also play. Her request was denied, although she could play as well as any of them. Her actions caused a stir. Not only was she riding astride the horse, and not sidesaddle as was the custom for women; she also was wearing riding pants! The ladies of Buringame were aghast. The Mothers Club passed a resolution that read: "Such unconventional trousers and clothes of the masculine sex are contrary to the hard and fast customs of our ancestors. It is immoral and wholly unbecoming a woman, having a bad effect on the sensibilities of our boys and girls."

Reports have it that many a sermon was preached about the brazenness of this particular socialite, but she just laughed it off. Her next sports conquest came in squash rackets. She took the game up in 1918 and was frequently invited to play at the Harvard Club although it was a "men's-only" organization. The first national championship for women was held in 1928, and Eleonora, although she was 46, was the first United States Women's champion. She competed in the tourney until 1950, when she was seventy years old, captained the United States women's international squash team, and became president of the Women's National Squash Rackets Association.

But squash, tennis, and polo were only a few of the sports in which Sears excelled. She popularized another sport and was the most dominant influence in still another.

During the 1920s, when Eleo was in her 40s, she began marathon walking, first to win a bet and later to publicize the need for physical fitness. On annual walks from Providence to Boston, a distance of 44 miles she created quite a scene as she strolled along the rural roads dressed in a short coat, felt hat, shirt, rolled down socks, and boots. She was usually escorted by a group of Harvard athletes and inevitably trailed by her chauffeur driving her private limousine. Sears moved briskly at a 12-minutes-per-mile pace. She later walked the 73 miles from Newport to Boston in seventeen hours and added the 43 miles from Fontainbleau to the Ritz Bar in Paris to her collection of triumphs.

Eleo's greatest love was for horses. She was a skilled steeplechase rider in horse shows and competed frequently in national and international competition. She raised some of the finest horses in the country and became a fixture at the National Horse Show. Eleonora supported the horse show financially during some bad times and provided the horses and money for the United States equestrian team. Her efforts to save the Boston mounted police brought news headlines. When a budget crunch threatened the existence of the Mounties, Eleo came up with the money and horses to continue this grand tradition.

A 1967 New York *Post* article said of Miss Sears: "She has had horses at the Garden every year since the National has been held. . . . Leafing back through 41 years of Garden programs, it is hard to find a show when a Sears horse did not win a blue ribbon. For many years, too, she rode them herself."

In several sports in which she did not formally compete she was competitive. She skated, sailed, and played golf well. Once she swam from

Newport's Bailey's Beach to First Beach, a distance of four and one-half miles. She skippered a yacht that defeated Alfred Vanderbilt's "Walthra." But that was not the first time a Vanderbilt could not catch her. In 1911 she was engaged to marry Harold S. Vanderbilt, the America's Cup yachtsman, but the romance ended, and Sears remained single all her life.

In addition to her sports activities, Eleonora remained active in the finest social circles. Her name was frequently on the "10-Best-Dressed" and "10-Best-Gowned" lists and, as might be expected, she was a graceful dancer. The Prince of Wales, who later became King Edward VIII, claimed that she was his favorite dance, squash, and tennis partner.

Eleonora Sears was vigorous until her death from leukemia in 1968 at Palm Beach, Florida, at age 87. Her obituary in the New York Times states: "Miss Sears. . . was acclaimed as one of the most striking sports personalities of her time. . . . She paved the way for women's entrance into sports."

Helen Herring Stephens

"The Missouri Express"
February 3, 1918–
Fulton, Missouri

Coach Burt Moore could not believe his eyes that fall afternoon in 1933. Every year the coach at Fulton High School in Missouri would get out his stopwatch and time entering freshmen in a 50-yard run. One big farm girl flew down the track. When the coach pushed the stop button, the watch read 5.8 seconds. The coach knew that the existing women's world record for the distance was 5.8, set by Elizabeth Robinson, the first woman to win an Olympic gold medal in track and field.

The strong fifteen-year-old girl was Helen Stephens, one of the first great all-around female athletes. Helen had a relatively short athletic career, but few careers have been more spectacular. That year Helen tied the record for the standing broad jump while practicing the event in gym class. Coach Moore began polishing her skills because he realized that Helen was a potential Olympic champion. He concentrated on sprinting because the prestige Olympic event for women was the 100-meter dash, although there was no sport with which Helen was not comfortable.

Helen Stephens, the first truly great woman sprinter (photo courtesy Helen Stephens).

Within two years, Helen Stephens, 17 years old, six feet tall, and a power-ful 135 pounds, was ready for big-time competition. She entered four events in the national Amateur Athletic Union (AAU) championships in St. Louis that year and won all four: the 50-meter dash, 200-meter dash, standing broad jump, and shot put. In the process she tied the 50-meter world record and established new world records at 200 meters and the standing broad jump. During the competition she accidentally started a feud with the best-known woman sprinter of that era, Stella Walsh. The bitterness lasted for years and had a bizarre ending.

Stella Walsh was born Stanislawa Walasiewicz in Rypin, Poland, in 1911. Her family emigrated to Cleveland within a few years of her birth, and she grew up as Stella Walsh. Before she was twenty Walsh broke the 11.0-seconds bar-rier for the women's 100-yard dash. She opted to represent Poland at the 1932 Olympic Games and won the 100-meter dash. But at the 1935 AAU meet, Stella met her match in Helen Stephens. Stephens easily beat Walsh at 50 yards and was completely surprised by all the congratulations she received. When told she had beaten the great Stella Walsh, the girl innocently asked, "Who is Stella Walsh?" When informed of the remark, Walsh referred to Stephens as "that greenie from the sticks."

Stephens's greatest moment in sports occurred during the 1936 Olympics. She was clearly the finest United States woman athlete on the Olympic team, probably the finest in the world. Six track and field events were held for women at the 1936 Games, the 100-meter dash, 4-by-100-meter relay, high jump, discus, javelin throw, and 80-meter hurdles. Each competitor could enter only three. Helen's best events were the sprint, standing broad jump, and shot put, but since the latter two were not on the program, she chose to compete in the sprint, discus, and relay. She could not find her form in the discus and finished tenth.

But she was ready for the 100-meter dash, blowing the competition away in a preliminary dash heat, winning by an incredible 10 yards in 11.4 seconds. The time shattered Walsh's existing Olympic record by a full second but the record was disallowed because of a following wind. Stephens was equally devastating in the finals, winning in world-record time of 11.5, a full two yards ahead of Stella Walsh, who ran her personal best, 11.7 seconds.

A second gold medal was gathered anchoring the United States team in their victory in the 4-by-100-meter relay. The American team may have been lucky. The favored German team, performing in front of Adolf Hitler, dropped the baton on the last pass. At the time Stephens was 10 yards behind the Ger-man runner, Ilse Dorffeldt, and might not have caught her, although with her momentum the Missourian might well have won at the tape anyway.

Helen Stephens was an instant celebrity and, as such, was introduced to

Adolf Hitler, the host of the 1936 Games, in his private box. The often-told story of Hitler's boorish behavior is best described by the runner: "Hitler comes in and gives me the Nazi salute. I gave him a good old Missouri handshake. He shook my hand, put his arm around me, pinched me, and invited me to spend a weekend with him." Helen had more important things to do.

Stephens continued to compete as an amateur through the rest of 1936 and most of 1937. On September 5, 1936, she stole the show at a special international track meet in Toronto. She opened by winning the 100-yard dash in 10.5 seconds, a world record, and came back with a 23.3 in the 220-yard dash. In that race, she spotted a field of Canada's best sprinters a headstart of twelve yards and passed them all out, winning by ten yards pulling away.

The Associated Press named Helen the "Best Woman Athlete of the Year" in 1936. The New York Times said of her selection: "Miss Stephens spectacular solo dash and the swift anchor leg she ran on the winning 400-meter Olympic relay quartet crowned previous performances at home where she won four national AAU championships. Just as she did in the vast stadium in Berlin before 100,000 spectators, Miss Stephens made a runaway of the poll."

In 1937 Stephens won national AAU titles at 50 and 200 meters and the shot put and retired after that season—never having been defeated in a running event! She competed for less than 30 months and in that time won more than 100 races, two Olympic gold medals, and 14 national AAU titles.

Helen had to earn a living, so like her idol, Babe Didrikson, she went into the barnstorming business. She ran a series of exhibition races against Jesse Owens and put together a touring professional basketball team. Helen was a fine basketball player, bowler, fencer, and swimmer.

During World War II, Stephens served with the Marine Corps and after the war was a librarian for the Defense Mapping Agency Aerospace Center in St. Louis for 25 years. When she retired, Helen returned to Florissant, Missouri, and helped coach sports at her alma mater, William Woods College.

When Stephens defeated Stella Walsh at the 1936 Olympic Games, some of Stella's supporters raised the charge that the big, strong girl from Missouri was in fact a man. The German officials issued a statement that they had given a sex test and she had passed. On December 4, 1980, Stella Walsh was accidentally caught in the middle of a holdup in Cleveland and was shot to death. On January 22, 1981, the Cayahoga County coroner's office issued the startling statement that was reported by the Associated Press as follows: "Stella Walsh who won a gold and silver medal in track competing as a woman in the 1932 and 1936 Olympic Games had male sex organs, according to an autopsy report released today. The report also said that Miss Walsh had no female sex organs."

In 1980, after a 43-year hiatus, Helen Stephens returned to competition in the senior Olympics. She won seven gold medals at the 1980 competition and seven gold and a bronze at the 1981 games. The streak remained intact; she still is undefeated in running competition.

Joyce Wethered
"Lady Heathcoat-Amory"
November 17, 1901–
Maldon, Surrey, England

When experts debate the identity of the greatest woman golfer who ever played, Joyce Wethered inevitably becomes part of the discussion. Those who saw her play argue that she certainly was among the best who ever teed up a golf ball.

Joyce Wethered was assuredly the finest British woman golfer of the 1920s and was universally considered the top golfer of her era. At the time there were few tournaments, but those she entered she dominated. She must be evaluated by the opinions of the people who saw her perform and were dutifully impressed.

Bobby Jones, the leading male golfer of Wethered's era played a round with her at the St. Andrew's course in Scotland just before he won the British Amateur title on his way to a golfing "grand slam." He said of her game:

> We played the Old Course from the very back, or the championship tees, and with a slight breeze blowing off the sea. Miss Wethered holed only one putt of more than five feet, took three putts rather half-heartedly from four yards at the seventeenth after the match was over, and yet she went around St. Andrews in 75. She did not miss one shot; she did not even half miss a shot; and when we finished, I could not help saying that I had never played golf with anyone, man or woman, amateur or professional, who made me feel so utterly outclassed. . . . I have no hesitancy in saying that, accounting for the unavoidable handicap of a woman's lesser physical strength, she is the finest golfer I have ever seen.

Even if Jones was being polite, that is strong praise from a person often considered to be one of the two or three best golfers of all time.

Joyce Wethered, considered by many to be the finest woman golfer ever, uses a fairway wood in this 1932 photo (photo courtesy Wide World Photos).

Henry Cotton, who won the British Open in 1934, 1937, and 1948, also had strong praise: "Joyce Wethered was a great golfer for she hit the ball as far as the average scratch player and with feminine grace. . .her putting and chipping were beautiful to watch. . .I do not think a golf ball has ever been hit except perhaps by Harry Vardon, with such a straight flight by any other person."

Wethered began playing tournament golf in 1920 when she was 19 years old and retired from serious competition at the ripe old age of 24. She staged one brief but spectacular comeback in 1929, but after that limited her play to mixed foursome competition. She won the English Ladies Championship for five consecutive years and participated in six British Women's Championships. She won four of these, was a runner-up once, and a semi-finalist once.

Her greatest moment in golf occurred when she came out of retirement in 1929 to face the upstart from "the colonies," American Glenna Collett, in the British Women's Championship. Both breezed through the preliminary rounds in match play in which the other 126 contestants were eliminated. The two greatest golfers of their day, Glenna Collett and Joyce Wethered, met head-to-head at St. Andrews in the finals. The English golfer, who had won their only previous match several years before, put away her American challenger, 3–1.

Wethered played golf casually but effectively after that. She loved the trout stream and growing roses at her country estate as much as the golf course. Wethered was tall, strong, and stately, and carried herself with the genteel, aloof demeanor expected of a woman of title, which she gained by marriage to Lord Heathcoat-Amory. She played regularly at the Worplesdon Tournament, which featured team match play with mixed foursomes. Lady Amory was an outstanding team player who won 8 of the 15 times she competed at Worplesdon, often carrying her male partner. Her husband was her partner several of the times she lost, and although he was good, he was not in the class of the other men players at that level of competition.

Her concentration on the course has been said to be the equal of Jack Nicklaus. She seldom practiced and was never aware of how effectively an opponent was playing. It was just she, the golf ball, and the flag. She once said, "If I could only bring myself to forget the excitement and importance of the match I was playing in, then I gave myself an infinitely better chance of reproducing my best form." She rarely lost concentration.

Said Henry Cotton: "In my time, no golfer has stood out so far ahead of his or her contemporaries as Lady Heathcoat-Amory. I am pleased to add to the world's acclaim my appreciation of this wonderful golfer—a figure of modesty and concentration, and an example to everybody."

Thirty-five More
Great Women Athletes

Tenley Emma Albright
"Dr. Tenley"
July 18, 1935–
Newton Centre, Massachusetts

Today she is known affectionately as "Dr. Tenley" and has had a successful career as a surgeon and pioneer in sports medicine. But Dr. Albright was a pioneer in another field nearly 40 years ago. She was the first American woman skater to win a world championship in figure skating and the first to win a gold medal at the Olympics.

In Newton Centre, Massachusetts, a well-to-do Boston suburb, Hollis Albright was a surgeon who loved sports and flooded his backyard each winter so that the neighborhood kids could have a safe skating pond. His daughter enjoyed ice skating, and by the time she was nine Tenley could trace figure-eights on the surface of the backyard pond.

When she was 11, however, the youngster contracted polio, a dreaded, paralyzing disease in those days before Dr. Jonas Salk's vaccine. Tenley's polio was a relatively mild strain that left her muscles weakened but not paralyzed. She had to learn to walk again on legs that wobbled and could not hold her 100-pound weight. She took up skating seriously at the Skating Club of Boston, partly to strengthen her legs, but mostly because she loved the sport. As she improved, her family arranged summer trips to places like Lake Placid and Denver so she could find more ice time. Albright won the United States Eastern Junior Championship in 1946 when she was 11 and went on to become the finest figure skater in the world.

As a blue-eyed, blonde 13-year-old, she became the United States novice champion and the National Junior Champion the following year. She won the United States Open Championship in 1952 at sixteen, her first of five, consecutive national titles, and finished second to Jeanette Altwegg of Great Britain at the Winter Olympics in Oslo. In 1953, she completed an impressive triple: winning the world title in Davos, Switzerland; the North American championship at Cleveland, Ohio, and the United States crown at Hershey, Pennsylvania.

Her victory at the world competition was ground-breaking since she was the first American woman to win that event, yet the decision of the seven judges was unanimous. She entered the free-skating phase with a wide lead from the compulsory figures competition and could have eased up in the free-skating

Tenley Albright, the Massachusetts marvel who became a respected surgeon (photo courtesy World Figure Skating Museum).

competition and still won. Albright, however, dazzled the audience. Her program and execution were both rated first by every judge.

Tenley Albright dominated women's figure-skating for a five-year period, as the chart below shows.

Championships

Year	United States	North American	World	Olympics
1952	won			second
1953	won	won	won	
1954	won		second	
1955	won	won	won	
1956	won		second	won

Tenley defeated Gundi Busch of West Germany for the world title in 1953 but Busch came back to defeat her in 1954. Frances Dorsey was runner-up to Albright in 1952. Carol Heiss, Albright's perennial challenger, finished second to her in the United States Nationals competition each year from 1953 through 1956. She defeated Heiss for the world title in 1955 but Heiss took the title in 1956. The two rivals were never too friendly, although they both publicly denied that animosity existed. Albright was four-and-one-half years older than Heiss, and when they competed head-to-head, she almost always had the upper hand. After Albright retired, Heiss was the top female figure skater in the world for the next five years.

Tenley Albright was at her best in school figures which, in her era, constituted 60 percent of the scoring. Competitors had to learn to trace 62 different figures on the ice, and six figures were chosen at random for each skater to execute in competition.

The rivalry during the 1956 season between Carol Heiss, sixteen, and Tenley Albright, twenty-one, created ice skating competition at its best. The highlight of Albright's career was winning the Olympic gold medal at Cortina, Italy, in 1956. She shook off the pain from a gash in her right ankle, the result of a skating accident ten days before, and was scored first by ten of the eleven judges. Sixteen days later, Heiss became the second-youngest woman to win the world figure-skating crown when she out-pointed Albright at the rink at Garmisch-Partenkirchen, the site of the 1936 Olympics. Heiss had six firsts and three seconds on the judges scorecards; Albright three firsts and six seconds. Compulsory figures held the key. Although leading after four figures, Albright faltered slightly on the last two figures to fall behind going into the free-skating program. Tenley skated first, to Offenbach's "Orpheus in Hades." She was nearly perfect. Carol skated to Adolphe Adams's "If I Were a King." The judges saw her as a 5.9; Albright a 5.8.

One month later in their rubber match for the season, Albright retained her United States crown by winning the compulsories and holding off Heiss's fiery challenge in the free skating. It was time for Albright to retire and concentrate on her medical studies.

"Dr. Tenley" still lives just outside Boston with husband, Gerald Blakeley, a real-estate developer. She is a general surgeon at Boston Deaconess Hospital and founder of Sports Medicine Resource, Inc., of Brookline, Massachusetts. Dr. Albright began her pre-med studies at Radcliffe College in 1953 and graduated from Harvard Medical School in 1960 when she was twenty-four. She was the team doctor for the United States Winter Olympic team in 1976. The American Academy of Achievement bestowed its highest honor on her that year, the Golden Plate Award. Her three daughters are fine skaters but were never figure-skating champions. Perhaps it is just as well; she would be a tough act to follow.

Joan Benoit Samuelson
"First Marathon Winner"
May 16, 1957–
Cape Elizabeth, Maine

Things never came easily for Joan Benoit. She became a runner after a broken leg abruptly cut short her budding career as a skier. Since then her running career has been a series of great victories and debilitating injuries.

Benoit was born in Cape Elizabeth, Maine, in 1957, the only girl in a family of four children. Her father, a retail clothing store owner, was an expert skier, so it was natural for young Joan to be drawn to the ski slopes that crown northern New England. Joan was becoming a fine competitive skier at the age of fifteen when she rammed a gate on a ski run at Pleasant Mountain, Maine. Her skiing was through for the season, so she resolved to work a little more diligently on the Cape Elizabeth High School track team that spring to help rehabilitate the leg. Track was almost incidental to Joan, who also played tennis and basketball in high school.

No instant Helen Stephens on the track, she had moderate local success in high school, running a mile in 5:15, and entered Bowdoin College in Maine to compete in field hockey and condition herself by running. Two factors held back her track progress: she did not take running seriously so she did not train sufficiently to excel, and there remained a bias against women in the distance races for which Joan was best suited.

For decades people thought that women were incapable of running long distances. When running events for women were first incorporated into the Olympic Games in 1928, the only individual events contested were the 100-meter dash and 800-meter run. Lina Radke of Germany set a world record for 800 meters that lasted for 16, but two women collapsed and needed assistance during the event. As a result, the International Amateur Athletic Federation declared that women would be banned from running races of more than 200 meters. Not until 1964 did the Olympics include a 400-meter run for women. During the 1960s some Amateur Athletic Union (AAU) officials were still saying that training for distance events might make a woman unable to bear children. As late as 1976, 1500 meters was the longest distance run by women in Olympic competition.

Benoit was only a fair middle-distance runner. She got as far as the trials for 1500 meters for the United States Olympic team in 1976, but she was not internationally competitive. Women began running longer distances at that time, and, to the surprise of many, they excelled at it. In 1967 Katherine Switzer attempted to run in the Boston Marathon but was ejected from the course. Within five years, women were allowed to run in marathons, but they were required to start ten minutes earlier than the men. This practice was ended when the women competitors staged a sit-in at the 1972 New York Marathon.

Benoit started maturing as a distance runner in 1976, after her freshman year at Bowdoin. She gave up field hockey because the lateral movement required for the sport was wreaking havoc on her knees. That summer she won the seven-mile road race at Falmouth, Massachusetts, a feat she accomplished six of the eight times she competed there. She continued to improve but was inconsistent until one cold and drizzly April day in 1979, when, as a relative unknown, she ran away with the Boston Marathon.

Boston was only her second attempt at the distance; she had entered a marathon in Maine on a lark and surprised herself by finishing second. But in Boston that day, she was unbeatable. Benoit took the lead at the 18-mile mark, near the notorious Heartbreak Hill, and coasted home in 2 hours, 35 minutes, 15 seconds, an American record for women. Instantly the darling of the Boston fans, who recognized her Bowdoin shirt and the Boston Red Sox cap she wore with the bill turned backwards, she did not care for the role of celebrity.

"I hated the publicity so much that I seriously considered giving up running so I would be left alone," she once said. Joan was on top of the running world, but tough luck would not permit her to remain there long.

Benoit missed the 1980 Boston Marathon because of an appendectomy,

Joan Benoit won the first Olympic marathon for women (photo courtesy Bowdoin College).

and ran a poor third in 1981. In between she ran well sometimes and poorly at other times. Late in 1981 a series of nagging injuries had to be repaired surgically. Bone spurs and scar tissue were removed from both heels. A torn Achilles tendon was repaired and both bursa sacs removed. The year 1982 began with both legs in casts. A prime candidate to be an athlete whose career blooms briefly but is quickly forgotten, Benoit realized it was time for a comeback or retirement.

Still recuperating from her operation, she was a broadcaster for the 1982 Boston Marathon, but slowly was getting into shape. In May, she won a 25,000-meter race and finished second to Grete Waitz in a mini-marathon. A series of road and cross country races had her ready for the 1983 Boston Marathon. The race was no contest. Joan ran 2:22.43 for a world record on the tough Boston course. Her time was more than two minutes faster than any woman had registered in a marathon.

Women distance runners saw 1984 as a monumental year; for the first time there would be an Olympic marathon for women. Several great runners, including Allison Roe of New Zealand, Rosa Mota of Portugal, and the two Scandinavians, Ingrid Kristiansen and Grete Waitz, had emerged in a few short years of competition. All were expected to join Benoit in the race to determine who was best.

Joan Benoit almost did not qualify for the first women's Olympic marathon. It took guts, to win the Olympic qualifier just 17 days after arthroscopic surgery on a knee, and then begin training for the race of her life.

On August 5, 1984, in Los Angeles, she pulled away from the pack at the three-mile mark and steadily ran away from the field. Surely she could not sustain the pace! But when she entered the Los Angeles Coliseum with a quarter-mile to go, Grete Waitz was a full one and one-half minutes behind in second place and Rosa Mota, subsequently the 1988 Olympic champion, was a distant third.

The following week, Joan married Scott Samuelson, whom she had met at Bowdoin. She continued to compete, and defeated both Ingrid Kristiansen and Rosa Mota in the 1985 Chicago Marathon which she ran in 2:21. Chronic heel problems then began to restrict her running. She attempted a comeback in 1988 at the New York Marathon and finished third. Even though she had won every marathon in which she competed since 1981, the third-place finish did not disappoint Joan. It was her first-ever New York appearance, and she realized that "I've been spending more time in therapy than running." But with leg, foot, back, and hip problems, her competitive running days seemed ended. However, in January 1990 Joan Benoit Samuelson, now a mother of two, was back in training. She won a mini-marathon in Norway in May of 1990 to show that she was most of the way back. Her nearest competitor was five minutes behind her.

Joan accomplished the ultimate in distance running with dogged determination in overcoming a seemingly endless plague of injuries. By winning the first Olympic marathon for women her place in sports is secure.

When not competing Joan Samuelson lives quietly in her beloved Maine and collects stamps, knits, picks blueberries, traps lobsters, square dances, enjoys family life, and runs in the fresh "down East" air.

Fanny Blankers-Koen winning the 80-meter hurdles at the 1948 Olympics (photo courtesy Netherlands Counsel-General).

Francina Blankers-Koen

"Fanny"
April 16, 1918–
Baarn, The Netherlands

Francina "Fanny" Blankers-Koen was the star of the 1948 London Olympic Games. Blankers-Koen, the mother of two children at the time, won four gold medals in the nine events in women's track and field. Her victories came in the 100- and 200-meter dashes, the 80-meter hurdles, and the 4-by-100-meter relay. In the relay, she came from fourth place to win on the anchor leg for Holland. She probably would have won a fifth gold medal if she had entered the long jump. The winning leap was 20 inches shorter than her existing world record. The outstanding series of performances were accumulated under some of the most adverse conditions ever seen in Olympic competition. It rained in London virtually every day that summer and Wembley Stadium, with its cinder track, was a quagmire for the entire competition.

Francina Koen was born in Baarn, the Netherlands, in 1918. Her father competed in local track meets as a shot putter and discus thrower. Fanny was a fine competitive swimmer, who switched to track and field when her coach suggested that the Netherlands had a surplus of women swimmers. She started running when she was 16, and at 18, qualified for the 1936 Dutch Olympic team. She finished sixth in the high jump and was a member of the Dutch 4-by-100-meter relay team that finished fifth. Soon after, she married her coach, Jan Blankers.

World War II stopped international competition for more than six years and interrupted her career during its peak years because the 1940 and 1944 games did not meet. But when the Olympics resumed in 1948, after a twelve-year lapse, Fanny held an incredible six world records: 100 yards, 80-meter hurdles, high jump, long jump, and two team relay events. The Netherlands was ravaged by almost five years of Nazi occupation, and the Dutch people needed a symbol of hope. The housewife became a national heroine as she trained for the first post-war Olympics. Each day she bicycled to practice with her two children sitting in a basket strapped over the rear wheel of her bike. The children played in the sand pits used for jumping events as mom worked out under the watchful eye of their dad, her coach.

The British press claimed a 30-year-old was "too old" to be a major factor in the competition. That notion soon evaporated. First she won the 100-meter dash and then the 80-meter hurdles. The hurdles finish was a nail-biter; after a terrible start she just caught Australian Shirley Strickland and local favorite Maureen Gardner at the tape. Then came her new Olympic record for 200 meters in a preliminary heat but she had reached the point of physical and emotional exhaustion. A pep talk from her husband-coach, encouraging her to win one for the children and her late parents, brought tears of determination. Just before she stepped onto the track for the finals, husband Jan reminded her, "Remember, Fanny, you're too old." She won by seven yards.

Blankers-Koen made the Dutch national anthem, "Wilhemus," a popular song in England that summer and returned to the Netherlands a conquering hero. She was paraded through the streets in a regal carriage drawn by four white horses. The government named a rose and gladiolus for her, and, like Reggie Jackson and Henry Aaron after her, a candy bar was named in her honor.

Blankers-Koen competed in the 1952 Olympics. Bothered by a leg injury, she hit the first two hurdles in the 80-meter finals and did not finish. As late as 1956, at age 38, she was still running 100 meters at 11.3 seconds, close to the existing world standard. Since retiring, she has lived a quiet life and watched her family grow.

Florence Mary Chadwick

"Trying to do . . . is what counts"
November 9, 1918–
San Diego, California

The opportunity for women to excel in swimming has been generally limited to the Olympic events. Two formidable competitors bucked the tide, both literally and figuratively, to make a name for themselves in long-distance swimming: Gertrude Ederle in the 1920s and Florence Chadwick in the 1950s.

Florence was born and raised in San Diego. Richard Chadwick was a police detective and later, with Florence's mother, Mary, a restaurant owner. Swimming competition began when Florence was six, and before she was 11 she became the first child to swim across the mouth of San Diego Harbor. She finished second to Eleanor Holm for the national backstroke championship at 50 yards at age 13, but she had to get away from the confines of the pool to show what she could really do.

Chadwick was a legend at the distance swimming events held in those days in Southern California and won the prestigious La Jolla 2.5-mile race ten times between 1929 and 1943. She was graduated from high school in 1936, attended college for three years studying law and business, but left school for show business.

Aquacades were one of the leading entertainment rages of the late 1930s and during World War II. Swimmer Eleanor Holm headlined the aquashow at the New York World's Fair. The swimming extravaganza film, featuring Esther Williams, was a mainstay of the Hollywood screen. Florence joined the United Service Organization (USO) efforts to entertain the troops during World War II as a producer and director of aqua shows for servicemen and veteran hospitals. In 1945 she appeared with Williams in a swimming spectacular movie and later became a swimming instructor at the La Jolla Beach and Tennis Club.

Because of the movie and instructor work, Florence was considered a professional, and therefore ineligible to compete in swimming meets. That was the impetus she needed to begin training to achieve her life-long ambition of swimming the English Channel. Florence obtained a position as a statistician for the Arabian-American Oil Company and went to Saudi Arabia where she could train in the choppy waters of the Persian Gulf. Florence swam both before and after work. On her days off she spent as long as 14 hours in the water. By 1950 she felt she was ready and headed for France to take on the Channel and challenge the record established by Ederle 24 years before. Both the Channel and the record succumbed to the powerful strokes of Chadwick.

On August 8, 1950, Florence Chadwick swam from Cape Gris-Nez in France to Dover, England, in 13 hours and 20 minutes to shatter Gertrude Ederle's record by one hour and 11 minutes. Ederle was the first woman to swim the channel, and although 11 women had succeeded in making the crossing after her, none had bettered her time.

Chadwick started out fighting the tide and swam a stroke per second to get into calmer water, where she eased to 48 strokes per minute. She virtually glided until she was within three miles of the British shore, at which point she encountered the ebbing tide. It took four hours to battle those last three miles, yet she strode from the water seemingly as refreshed as she was when she left France. As she waded ashore in England, she nonchalantly said to the waiting newsmen, "I feel fine. I am quite prepared to swim back." The Channel crossing was the first of many monumental swims for the powerful Californian.

The English Channel is easier to swim from France to England than from England to France because of the prevailing tides. Chadwick swam the Channel the hard way three times, in 1951, 1953, and 1955. Her 1951 crossing was made in heavy fog and adverse tidal conditions. By 1953, she was so adept at Channel crossings that she swam it four times in a five-week period. Her 1955 crossing was done in 13 hours and 55 minutes, which cut 11 minutes off the existing men's record. She was 35 years old at the time.

In between Channel swims, Chadwick became the first woman to swim the twenty-one miles from Catalina Island to the California mainland in September of 1952. Her time, 13 hours and 47 minutes, was the best time for any swimmer at that time. The existing record, established by Canadian, George Young, was set in 1927. In 1953, she also swam a round trip across the Strait of Gibraltar and conquered both the Dardanelles and the Bosporus.

Florence Chadwick towels off after a grueling practice session (photo courtesy International Swimming Hall of Fame).

Florence Chadwick, like most distance swimmers, had her disappointments. The Straits at Juan DeFuca and Lake Ontario defeated her, and she did not make it across the Irish Sea in 1960, her last monumental effort.

Florence is five feet, six inches tall and weighs 140 pounds. Doctors said that she was "unusually resistant to cold." President Dwight Eisenhower, acknowledging her fame and good looks said, "I'd know you anywhere," and Gypsy Rose Lee, considered a fine beauty in her day, called her "the most beautiful woman in sports."

After retiring from swimming, Chadwick spent ten years making public appearances at sport shows, swim schools and on radio and television. In 1969 she began a new and successful career as Wall Street stockbroker.

Most of Florence's records have been broken since most swimmers now use radar to plot a course that shortens the distance from one point to another. But Florence Chadwick is still universally recognized as the finest distance swimmer of all time.

The late Johnny Weissmuller, who made his own mark as possibly the strongest swimmer ever and certainly the one who did the most to popularize the sport, evaluated Chadwick as "the greatest woman swimmer of all time—maybe of either sex—and it's time she got credit for it."

"If I had the chance to relive my life, I would do it all again because it is trying to do what you badly want to do that counts," was her own comment on a life spent doing what she wanted very much to do.

Nadia Comaneci

"The Perfect 10"
November 12, 1961–
Onesti, Romania

The "Perfect 10"? That best describes, not Bo Derek, but Nadia Comaneci, a tiny 14-year-old gymnast from Romania. Nadia did things in gymnastics that had never been done before, and did them perfectly. Her standards have yet to be matched.

Americans, generally, would have a difficult time putting a finger on Romania on a map. Many who can are able to because Nadia put Romania "on the map" for much of the world.

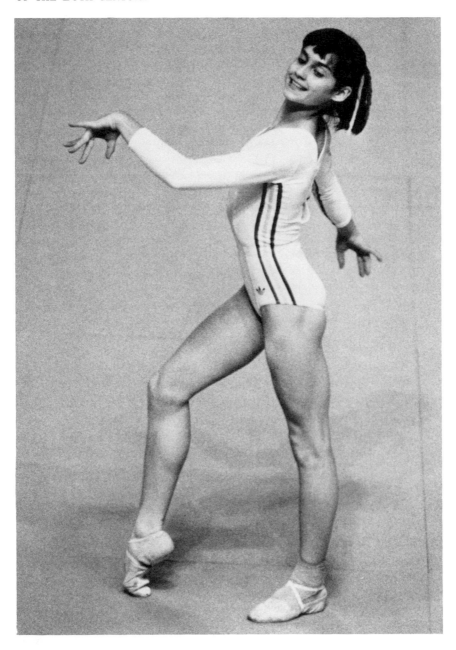

Nadia Comaneci shows her pixyish "perfect 10" form (photo courtesy International Gymnast).

When the Iron Curtain was lowered and the separation of the Western democracies from the Eastern socialist states was cemented by the Berlin Wall, the Soviet bloc countries realized they had an identity crisis. The Soviets, and later the East Germans, concentrated on sports as a way of showing the rest of the world that the Communist system was superior. During the 1972 Olympics a petite Soviet gymnast, Olga Korbut, captivated the world with her athletic skill. Korbut was good, but her less charismatic teammate, Ludmilla Tourisheva, was better. The Western world had no gymnast who could come close to these stars from the East.

Yet it was another little girl who in April of 1975 impressed the West more than all the tanks and missiles the Eastern countries could muster. Nadia Comaneci, still 13 and described as solemn and doe-eyed, appeared with the Romanian gymnastic team at Wembley in England in the first Champions-All Tournament and performed miracles on both the uneven bars and the beam. Cynics mentioned "beginner's luck," and the experts were still not impressed when Comaneci went on to win the All-Around title in the 1975 European championships in Norway. The Olympics would tell the full measure of the athlete, the skeptics chortled.

Gymnastic competition in the Olympics is arduous and complex. The competitors first vie in team competition in four events: the vault, beam, uneven bars, and floor exercises. In each category, there are both compulsory and optional exercises. The person with the highest score in this competition is awarded the All-Around championship medal. The best six finishers in each event proceed to a final individual competition.

Gymnastics fans anticipated that women's competition would be a classic confrontation between the "old guard," represented by Tourisheva, and new challengers Korbut and Nellie Kim; all were from the Soviet Union. Tourisheva had won the All-Around championship in the 1972 Olympics as a 19-year-old, although Olga Korbut, the four-feet-eleven-inch, 85-pound 17-year-old from Byelorussia, had stolen the show despite finishing seventh. Korbut was great, and her performance captured the attention of the world television audience. But she had a disastrous time on the uneven bars and dropped dramatically in the standings. Nadia was expected to be just another contender.

Comaneci, however, scored the first perfect score of 10 in the Olympic gymnastic competition when she executed her compulsory exercise on the uneven bars. Before the competition was over, she registered seven 10s, four on the bars and three on the beam. Her competition were considered unbeatable, but perfect scores beat the unbeatable. She won the All-Around championship, scoring 79.275 out of a possible 80 points. Although 14-year-old Nadia could not project the showmanship of the bouncy Korbut, she brought down the house with her spectacular floor exercise, performed to the tune of "Yes Sir, That's My Baby." In the individual events, she won gold medals in both the balance beam and the uneven bars, and a bronze medal for the floor exercise. The Romanian team also won the silver medal for team competition. At fourteen she was the youngest person ever to win an Olympic gold medal in gymnastics.

Nadia was born on November 12, 1961, in Onesti, Romania. Her father was an auto mechanic, her mother a hospital worker. Bela Karolyi, the famous gymnastics coach who later defected to the U.S., discovered Nadia romping in a school playground when she was six and knew he had a gifted athlete on his hands. She began training immediately, was in competition by the time she was seven, won the Romanian national junior title at eight, and began international competition at eleven. Coach Karolyi maintains that six characteristics made her a champion: physically she had strength, speed, and agility; mentally she possessed courage, intelligence, and concentration.

Comaneci's performances were mechanically perfect, yet she seldom smiled. What she lacked in charisma, she more than made up for with her calm confidence and complete fearlessness while attempting difficult and dangerous maneuvers. She had the uncanny ability to shut out the distracting thought that millions of people were watching her. Rod Hill, the former manager of the U.S. Women's Olympic team said Comaneci "is the epitome of perfection." At her peak in 1976, she was just under five feet tall and weighed eighty-six pounds. One sportswriter described her style this way: "She stunned the judges not only with double somersaults and twists, but also with an uncommon consistency and stability even in her most difficult moves. . . . She had classical style with its emphasis on maturity and ladylike grace."

The gymnast returned to the 1980 Olympics in Moscow and finished second in the All-Around competition to Yeleva Davydova of the Soviet Union. The consensus among many neutral observers was that she was the victim of a "home town" decision. The Soviet and Polish judges awarded her only a 9.8 on the last event, the balance beam. Her final score of 79.075 was just slightly below Davydova's 79.15. In the individual events, Comaneci won the gold in the beam and floor exercises and added two silver medals to her collection.

Comaneci retired after the 1980 competition and coached in relative obscurity in Romania. She made a brief appearance as a coach with the Romanian national team at the 1984 Olympics, the same year her life story was dramatized as a television movie.

In December of 1989 a very grown-up, 28-year-old woman came through what was left of the Iron Curtain, seeking a prize more precious than Olympic gold—her personal freedom. Nadia, who in 1976 was named a "Hero of Soviet Labor" by her homeland, sought asylum in the U.S. Although she was a national hero, Romanian officials curtailed her foreign travel primarily because they were afraid she might defect. Her activities were always closely monitored; her country's officials would not allow her to be a judge at international competitions. She left her family, medals, sports car, prestigious apartment, and doll collection behind. The former "mechanical doll" sought the opportunity to be the best that she could be. In gymnastics, no one was ever better.

Maureen Connolly
"Little Mo"
September 17, 1934–June 21, 1969
San Diego, California

For too few years, the world of women's tennis thrilled to the performances of a young Californian who played the game as well as it has ever been played. Allison Danzig, the premier American tennis commentator, described Maureen Connolly as "this little blond scrapper with the bobbing head, twinkling toes, and the killer instinct on the court of a Jack Dempsey in the ring," Danzig compared Connolly with "no one less than Helen Wills." She was dubbed "Little Mo" by Nelson Fisher of the San Diego Times Union because her fire power rivaled that of "Big Mo," the battleship Missouri.

Connolly became a name in tennis when she won the United States singles championship at Forest Hills in 1951 at the age of 16. In that tournament, Maureen defeated Doris Hart, 6–4, 6–4, in the semifinals and then beat Shirley Fry, 6–3, 1–6, 6–4, in a thriller to take the title. But Little Mo was just at the beginning of a fabulous streak.

In 1952, she won at Wimbledon in her first attempt, and at age seventeen was the youngest winner there since Lottie Dod took the championship as a fifteen-year-old in 1887. Maureen successfully defended at Forest Hills that year, easily defeating Doris Hart. Hart and Fry were the two best women tennis players in the world at that time. Hart had won at Wimbledon in 1951 and later won back-to-back United States championships in 1954 and 1955. Fry won both the United States and All-England championships in 1956, and, as a doubles team, Fry and Hart won the United States championship four consecutive times from 1951 through 1954.

Maureen Connolly shows off her 1954 Wimbledon trophy (photo courtesy San Diego Historical Society).

In 1953 Connolly became the first woman to complete the "grand slam" of tennis, winning the national championships of Australia, France, Great Britain, and the United States. She did not lose a match that year. In fact, from September 1951 until July 1954, when she won her third consecutive Wimbledon title, she lost only to Beverly Baker Fleitz in the La Jolla Beach and Tennis Club International's semi-final in 1964. Fleitz, an ambidextrous player who switched the racket from hand to hand as the shot dictated, caught Connolly after a three-month layoff and trounced her, 6–0, 6–4. Maureen had no excuses. She commented, "Everything I hit at her she sent back. She was just too good, too good."

From the time she turned 16 until her premature retirement at 19, Connolly lost only four matches. The following table shows her record in grand slam tournaments. Blank spaces are events in which she did not complete.

Year	France	England	Australia	United States
1951				won
1952		won		won
1953	won	won	won	won
1954	won	won		retired from competition

As shown above, Connolly won every grand slam event she entered—nine of them before she was 20. Tennis immortal Vinnie Richards said of her game, "She hits her forehand harder and better than any woman in history."

Tragedy struck Maureen Connolly just before she was to compete in the 1954 United States Nationals Singles championship at Forest Hills. Maureen was an avid horsewoman and an excellent rider. She was riding a gift horse, a jumper named Colonel Mayberry, in San Diego, when the horse reared when frightened by the noise of a sanitation department truck it was passing. The horse fell against the truck, pinning and crushing Connolly's right leg. Extensive surgery never repaired the leg sufficiently for her to become competitive in tennis again.

Born in San Diego, her father, a naval officer, and her mother, a musician, divorced when Maureen was three. She was raised by her mother and an aunt. She grew up with two loves, tennis and horses. A natural left-hander, she switched to playing right-handed in high school. She won 70 tournaments by the time she was 16.

Her trademark on the court was concentration. She lacked a powerful serve but developed accuracy in her shots that has yet to be equaled. She never seemed to be upset when a match was going badly, but continued to play with the calm confidence and determination that made her a winner.

As a teenager her philosophy was that "I always seem to have a wonderful time. And even though tennis is a big part of my life, it isn't everything. Really, I love tennis, sure. But I feel that if it keeps me from sleeping or eating or having fun, it isn't worth it. I'd give it up."

After she retired from tennis, Maureen married Norman Brinker, an Olympic horseman, raised two children, Cindy and Brenda, and taught tennis. In 1969, at the age of 34, she lost a three-year bout to cancer.

Maureen Connolly was the first woman to win the tennis grand slam, a feat not duplicated until Margaret Smith Court did it seventeen years later. The Associated Press called her "Woman Athlete of the Year" for three consecutive years, 1952, 1953, and 1954. In 1968, she was elected to the Tennis Hall of Fame at Newport, Rhode Island. She placed third in the Associated Press's 1952 "Woman-of-the-Year" poll. Queen Elizabeth of England and Mamie Eisenhower nosed her out.

Margaret Smith Court
"The Private Life"
July 16, 1942–
Albury, New South Wales, Australia

Australia has long been known for its great tennis players. Australian men such as Ken Rosewall, Lew Hoad, Ashley Cooper, Rod Laver, Neale Fraser, Roy Emerson, Fred Stolle, and John Newcombe dominated tennis for decades. Margaret Court was the first Australian woman tennis player to be known internationally.

Tall, lean, rangy, and strong, in many respects, she did not have the tools to be great at the game. She was not particularly quick on the court. Throughout her career she had to fight the jitters every time she had a big match. Worse yet, she hated to travel. Yet no one worked harder; Court literally made herself a champion by consistent effort.

Personable on a one-to-one basis but shy in public, Court often found the post-match interviews the most difficult part of a tennis tournament. Sportswriters labeled her bland and introverted because she never gave them the quotable quotes they needed to file their story. Her record, however, speaks for itself.

Margaret Court competing in Australia in 1976 (photo courtesy Australian Foreign Affairs and Trade Department).

Margaret Smith won the All-England tournament at Wimbledon three times and was the first Australian woman to win the title. She won the Women's Singles championship of the United States five times, the French Open four, and took her own nation's title on ten occasions, for a total of 22 grand slam singles wins, a record that still stands. She also won the national titles of South Africa four times, Germany three, India twice, and Canada and Iceland once each. She was rated the number-one women's tennis player in the world in 1962, 1963, 1964, 1965, 1969, 1970, and 1973.

Her record in grand slam events:

Year	Australian	French	British	United States
1961	won			
1962	won	won		won
1963	won		won	
1964	won	won		
1965	won		won	won
1966	won			
1967		(temporarily retired)		
1968				won
1969	won	won		won*
1970	won	won	won	won
1971	won			
1972		(began raising a family)		
1973	won	won		won

*In 1969 Smith Court won both the United States Women's Singles title and the United States Open Title. These were different tournaments in 1968 and 1969.

Margaret Smith Court had two seasons in which she played tennis as well as anyone in the history of the game. In 1970 she became the second woman to complete a tennis grand slam when she won the titles of Australia, France, Britain, and the United States. Perhaps an even more remarkable accomplishment was her winning three grand slam events in 1973, shortly after the birth of her first child. That year she lost at Wimbledon to Chris Evert in the semi-final round but won a total of 18 tournaments.

Her greatest victory was in her grand slam year when she defeated Billy Jean King at Wimbledon, 14–12, 11–9, a 46-game marathon that is still the longest women's match on record at Wimbledon. She played that match with a sprained ankle.

Smith Court also excelled at doubles. She completed a grand slam of the doubles titles in 1963 with partner Kenneth Fletcher to add to her total of 63 grand slam titles. Bud Collins, the Boston sportswriter and tennis mavin, says, "For sheer strength of performance and accomplishment there has never been a tennis player to match Margaret Smith Court."

Margaret Smith was born in 1942 at Albury, New South Wales. Her home was across the street from the Border Lawn Tennis Association where her love affair with tennis first developed. Margaret swept the courts, painted the net posts and chalked the lines at the club as a youngster in exchange for playing time and instruction from the local professional. Her father was an ice cream maker at the local butter factory.

An all-around athlete, in school she was captain of her basketball and softball teams and loved to run almost as much as she loved tennis. She became a strong runner and at one point trained to represent Australia at the 1964 Olympic games at either 400 or 800 meters. She abandoned the attempt when she realized that she was losing some of the lateral movement she needed to stay at the top of her tennis game.

Smith won her first Australian national title in 1960 when she was 17, but her first tour in competition outside of Australia in 1961, as part of a national team, was a disaster because she was bullied by the Australian tennis officials. She was polite and vulnerable to the petty tyrants so often encountered in amateur officialdom, but when put in a corner, she fought back like a tigress.

The following year, she had her own sponsors and was able to compete without the political haggling. In her second tour, she won the Italian, Swiss, and French national championships but was upset by upstart American Billy Jean Moffitt in the first round of Wimbledon play. Margaret trounced Billy Jean the following year.

Most experts agree that Smith Court had less natural ability than most top tennis players. Fred Perry, the famous tennis teacher, said, "What she has accomplished has been done through sheer hard work." She was the first woman to use weights in training and was proud that she could lift 150 pounds. Billy Jean King called her "The Arm" because of her strength, recalling, "It was awesome to watch Margaret walk on the court. . . . She had this big heavy forehand that was like a slap and a great, low first serve. She was the first consummate athlete to play the game." The two players differ about Smith Court's role in the feminist revolution that took place during her prime. King, the more outspoken feminist, is her greatest admirer: "She is women's lib in action; even though she doesn't seem to realize it. She earns the bread and her husband babysits." Playing down her own importance, she shyly says, "I'm just a wife and mother who plays tennis."

But she always was torn between the glare of the tennis spotlight and her personal privacy. She married Barrymore Court, a successful wool broker and yachtsman, in 1967 and opened a boutique in Perth, Australia. But as much as she loved the quiet life, she could not stay away from the game for long. When she came back she was the best in the world, yet twice she took leaves from tennis to have children.

Court finally put the rackets away permanently in 1975 and enjoys the peace and quiet of just being a private citizen, albeit, still one of the most famous women in Australia.

Mary Teresa Decker

"Four-phase Career"
August 4, 1958–
Bunnvale, New Jersey

Mary Decker's track career has been a lesson in determination. Through innumerable injuries and keen disappointments she has consistently returned to perform at the world-class level. In a sport where short careers are the norm, Decker has competed in four decades.

During the early 1970s a 15-year-old, 100-pound newcomer took on the finest women middle-distance runners in the world and consistently beat them. Twenty years later she was still a world-class runner. Much happened in between in a career that progressed through four phases.

She was "Little Mary Decker" when she started, a great young runner who thrilled the spectators with her spectacular come-from-behind finishes. Mary won her first race in 1969 when she was eleven and discovered that she was not only good at running, but she enjoyed it. In retrospect, that may have been the cause of later health problems, for she probably ran too much when she was young. Mary ran a 4:55 mile when she was thirteen and at fourteen she toured Europe with the United States team and turned in an impressive series of international victories. She set her first world record when she was fifteen and ran 1000 yards indoors in 2:26.7 at Los Angeles in January of 1974. Her outdoor season that year was climaxed by a victory at 800 meters in the United States-Soviet Union track meet. But then injuries set in, and Decker was out of serious competition from mid–1974 until mid–1977.

The first injury was a stress fracture in the ankle, complicated by severe shin splints. The shin problem would not go away, and no doctor seemed

Mary Decker winning the 1988 Fifth Avenue Mile (photo courtesy Wide World Photos).

capable of curing it. Not until 1977 did she undergo an operation to correct her overdeveloped calf muscles. Meanwhile the 1976 Olympics passed, where she would have been a favorite for a medal.

Decker's second career lasted from the spring of 1978 until August of 1980. Now in her 20s and fully grown to five foot six and 105 pounds, a half foot taller and 25 pounds heavier than "Little Mary Decker," she resumed her career as a world-class runner, establishing a new world record for the indoor 1000 yards in 1978. She was a Pan Am gold medalist at 1500 meters in 1979 and ran a world record 4:21.7 mile in early 1980. More world records were set at 1500 meters and 800 yards indoors, despite continued tendenitis, sciatic nerve problems, and a sprained tendon in her left foot. She qualified for the 1980 United States Olympic team by winning the 1500 meter run at the trials, only to be frustrated by the United States's boycott of the Moscow Olympics. A second operation to correct her calf problems ended the second phase of Mary's career.

After an injury-induced two-year layoff, Decker was back on the track and healthy in 1982 and at the peak of her career. She ran as well and consistently in 1982 and 1983 as any woman track athlete ever, establishing an unbroken streak of victories that continued into 1984. One record after another fell. In 1982 Decker set world marks for the mile indoors and 2000 and 3000 meters outdoors. Then it was the world record at 5000 meters, followed by the 1500-meter mark. The first time she entered a 10,000-meter race she established a new world standard 42 seconds faster than the previous record. She won the Jesse Owens Award in 1982 as the nation's finest track athlete and was proclaimed "Amateur Sportswoman of the Year" by the Women's Sports Foundation. She also won the Sullivan Award as the nation's finest amateur athlete.

The following year was equally brilliant. At the end of the 1983 campaign she held every indoor world record for distances from 800 meters through two miles and the outdoor world marks from 800 meters through 10,000 meters. A healthy Mary Decker would finally get her chance to compete in the Olympics.

The most dramatic event in her career occurred during the 1984 Olympic Games. Decker, then 26, earned her way to the final of the 3000-meter run. She got off well and controlled the pace, staying comfortably ahead of her 18 year-old rival, Zola Budd, a South African running for Great Britain. As they came down the straightaway with slightly more than three laps to go, Budd made her move to pass Decker. As Budd inched into the lead, Decker's right foot hit Budd's left ankle and Mary went sprawling to the track. She recalled that, "when I fell, I tried to get up. That's when I felt the muscle." She was assisted from the track in tears. Later she said, "Zola Budd tried to cut in without being actually ahead. I should have pushed her, but if I had, the headlines would have been 'Mary pushes Zola.'" Zola was disqualified for the infraction but later was reinstated and placed second.

Decker temporarily retired from competition after that to begin raising a family. Her daughter, Ashley Lynn, was born in May 1986 and Mary was back competing in May 1988. She made the 1988 Olympic team and competed well but was not a medal winner. She had yet to recapture her prepregnancy form.

Mary competes in the 1990s, and her earnings from track appearances and endorsements is well into the six-figure range. She has had a splendid and courageous career and is unquestionably the finest American woman middle-distance runner of all time.

Kornelia Ender
"Fastest Swimmer in the World"
October 25, 1958–
Plausen, East Germany

Kornelia Ender was one of the best athletes the East German athletic system ever produced. The swimming world became aware of her at the 1972 Summer Olympics in Munich when the 13-year-old youngster won three silver medals. She finished second to Australia's Shane Gould's world record performance in the 200-meter individual medley. Ender's time was .09 second off the existing world record. She anchored East Germany's 4-by-100-meter freestyle relay team which finished second to a world-record setting Soviet Union team. Kornelia then swam the last leg, the freestyle, in the 4-by-100-meter medley relay, finishing second to the United States. It was one of the most striking performances by a 13-year-old in the history of sports. Kornelia had served notice that she intended to be the best swimmer of her generation. The following year, the 14-year-old youngster was the fastest swimmer in the world.

On July 13, 1973, Kornelia Ender broke Shane Gould's world record for the 100-meter freestyle in 58.25. She had lowered the 100-meter mark to 56.22 by the time she was 16, and shattered the record eight more times. That year, 1973, a Swimming World Championship meet was held for the first time. The games, held in Belgrade, became a showcase for Kornelia. She won four gold and one silver medal with individual victories in the 100-meter free-style and butterfly and team firsts in the freestyle and medley relays. Her silver medal was won in the 200-meter individual medley.

Ender won four golds at the European Championships in Vienna in 1974; in 1975 it was four golds and a silver at the world meet at Cali. Between 1973 and 1975 she established 15 world records. The scene was set for the highpoint of her career, the 1976 Montreal Olympics.

Much has been written about the fantastic progress made by the East German swimmers during the mid–1970s. In 1972, the East German team did not win a single gold medal at the Olympics. Yet in 1973, led by Ender, they were the strongest team at the World Championships. In 1976, they won 11 of the 13 Olympic swimming events. "Robots, who trained on steroids" was the accusation, a charge never substantiated. East Germany pioneered most of the early studies in sports medicine. It quickly surpassed larger countries, such as the Soviet Union and the United States, in getting athletes into peak physical condition. East German trainers and doctors became experts in lactic acid buildup, increased oxygen levels, and nutrition. They introduced scientifically-controlled weight lifting into their women's programs.

East German swimming officials spotted Ender as she swam on a family vacation. Her parents encouraged her to swim to correct an orthopedic problem. She attended a special school where sports training was given equal status with studies. Significantly, she began weight-lifting before she was ten years old.

Kornelia Ender was a muscular, five-foot ten-inch, 154 pounds at her competitive best. She was a stronger, faster swimmer than her competitors.

She won her usual "four golds and a silver" at Montreal to run her career total to eight Olympic medals. The four gold medals were more than any woman swimmer had won previously. She was the first East German woman to win an Olympic gold medal in swimming.

Ender began her Montreal victory parade by winning the 100-meter freestyle in world-record time of 55.65; the tenth and last time that she reestablished that standard. Next it was a world record 1:54.26 for the 200-meter freestyle, again breaking her own mark. She added the 100-meter butterfly gold to her collection, this time only equaling the world record. She completed her sweep by anchoring the East German 4-by-100-meter freestyle relay team as it set a world mark and swam the freestyle leg in the 100-meter medley relay in a second-place finish. She retired after her Olympic triumphs.

A poignant moment occurred during her triumphal performance at Montreal when she met her grandmother, who left East Germany for the United States when Kornelia was five months old. The reunion was set up with the

Kornelia Ender, the greatest of the East German women swimmers (photo courtesy International Swimming Hall of Fame).

permission of the East German officials, who kept a watchful eye on the grandmother and granddaughter during their 45-minute chat. The German government was deathly afraid that the showpiece of their athletic program might defect to the West, which would have been a damaging blow to the regime.

Ender was voted "World Swimmer of the Year" in 1973, 1975, and 1976. She was inducted into the International Swimming Hall of Fame in 1981.

Genetics experts have conjectured for decades about what would result if the finest male and female athletes in a field married. That has happened several times: skaters Carol Heiss and David Jenkins; track stars Florence Griffith and Al Joyner; and Kornelia Ender and Roland Matthes. Matthes, like Kornelia, won eight Olympic medals in swimming. Someday soon we may be reading about the accomplishments of their daughter, Francesca.

Christine Marie Evert

"America's Sweetheart"
December 21, 1954–
Ft. Lauderdale, Florida

The essence of success is timing. Chris Evert emerged as a tennis star precisely when women's professional tennis was coming of age and needed a personality everyone could love. Evert was perfect.

Chris Evert grew up with a tennis racket in her hand. Her father was a teaching tennis professional at the Holiday Park Tennis Center in Fort Lauderdale, Florida. He attended Notre Dame University on a tennis scholarship and won the United States National Indoor Championship in 1940 and the Canadian Singles Championship in 1947. Chris and her two brothers and two sisters were playing tennis from the time they were six.

In the fall of 1970, when Evert was still 15, she defeated the great Margaret Smith Court in a tournament in North Carolina. Smith Court had just become the second woman in history to record a grand slam, winning the national titles of Australia, France, Great Britain and the United States. Evert won the United States Junior Tennis Championship in both 1970 and 1971.

Known in the press as "Chrissie" she became nationally known in 1971 when, as a 16-year-old, she entered the United States Open Championship with her pony tail flying and advanced as far as the semifinals, losing to the eventual champion, Billy Jean King. Chris lost the tournament but won the acclaim of tennis fans, who fell in love with her clean-cut image. When some of the other women in the tournament complained about how much the galleries favored Evert, King, ever the businessperson, advised, "The other girls should worry about their own little worlds and about the whole sport. This is a 16-year-old kid who's beating the best people in the world. It's beautiful."

Chris Evert began winning grand slam tennis tournaments in 1974 when she won both the French and British Open Championships. She was the Associated Press "Female Athlete of the Year" in 1974 and 1975. She dominated women's tennis in the late 1970s and competed effectively throughout most of the 1980s. Evert was rated number-one in the world for four consecutive years from 1975 through 1978. During the 1970s she won 93 titles in the 155 tournaments, compiling a 659–61 record. Chris retired from competition at the end of the 1989 season. For the 13 years between 1974 and 1986 she won at least one grand slam event every year. Her victory record in the Australian, French, British, and United States Championships during this period is:

Year				
1974		French	British	
1975		French		United States
1976			British	United States
1977				United States
1978				United States
1979		French		
1980		French		United States
1981			British	
1982	Australian			United States
1983		French		
1984	Australian			
1985		French		
1986		French		

Evert was at her best in United States Open play; she compiled a U.S. Open record of 101–13, a .890 winning percentage, and won the title five times from 1973 until 1979.

Some thought her game boring to watch. Opponents were frequently frustrated by the monotonous accuracy of her volleys. She was a clay court specialist who could win on other surfaces but was virtually unbeatable in her own environment, specializing in playing the baseline. Evert won 125 consecutive matches on clay before falling to Tracy Austin at the 1979 Italian Open. She won 24 tournaments in that string. Evert was the United States clay court champion in 1972, 1973, 1974, 1975, 1979, and 1980. She also was devastating in international team play, playing for the United States against Great Britain's best on six victorious Wightman Cup teams with an individual record of 16 and 0. She won each of 14 matches in International Federation Cup play.

"Chrissie" quickly piled up the earnings, because she arrived on the tennis

Chris Evert, one of the finest competitors in the history of tennis (photo courtesy Carol L. Newsom Associates/Virginia Slims).

scene when women were beginning to receive acceptable purses. She turned professional in 1972 as a 17-year-old high school graduate. Four years later she was the first million-dollar winner in women's tennis. She earned more than $7 million in prize money before she retired.

Standing five feet, five inches tall and weighing 115 pounds in her prime, she compensated for a lack of power by developing a two-handed backhand swing that delivered the ball with consistent accuracy. Her strategy was to play at the backline and wait for her opponent to make a minuscule mistake. When it happened, she pounced. She developed the on-court demeanor of Helen Wills and Maureen Connolly; she seldom showed emotion as she methodically devoured her opponents. She earned the nicknames, "The Ice Queen" and "The Little Ice Maiden."

Off-court, Evert livened the circuit as a tease and a clown and one of the more active practical jokers among the professionals. She has been one of the most popular women on the touring circuit.

Chris was married to British tennis professional John Lloyd from 1979 until 1987. Her four-year romance with Jimmy Connors early in her career might have soured because it was so thoroughly covered in the tabloids.

Evert was the Women's Tennis Association's "Player of the Year" in 1981 and was elected that same year to the Women's Sports Foundation's Hall of Fame.

Peggy Gale Fleming
"America's Shy Bambi"
June 27, 1948–
San Jose, California

The U.S. Olympic team performed poorly at the 1968 winter games at Grenoble, France. Only one American star shone brightly, a brunette figure skater from Colorado by way of California. Peggy Fleming dazzled the figure-skating competition judges with her pure grace to earn the United States its only gold medal. A few weeks later Fleming added the world championship to her collection and promptly retired from amateur competition.

Like so many amateur athletes, Peggy Fleming's story is that of a family's sacrifice to give a potentially great athlete the opportunity to excel. Peggy was born in San Jose, California, in 1948. Her father was a pressman who changed jobs frequently. Peggy grew up in a succession of cities, from Cleveland, Ohio, to Pasadena, California. Fleming first skated at nine and competed at 11. At 12 she was the Pacific Coast juvenile figure-skating champion; California is famous for its athletes, but the West Coast is hardly the hotbed of figure skating. Peggy improved to the point where she won the United States championship in 1964, at the age of 15. But she was really not that good yet,

Peggy Fleming, poetry in motion (photo courtesy World Figure Skating Museum).

since competition in the United States was weak. The entire national team—18 figure skaters—was killed in an airplane crash near Brussels, Belgium, in 1961. Peggy competed in the 1964 Olympics at Innsbruck, Austria, and finished sixth in her first international competition. But her potential was obvious. Robert Daley, writing of her 1964 performance in the *New York Times* said, "She is a tall, slender girl and there is wondrous lightness to the way she lands after leaps and spins. She fell once but bounced back up undismayed. She gives every indication of being a champion of the future."

Fleming went on to win the United States title again in 1965 and finished second to Petra Burka at the North American championships. At that point her family moved to Colorado Springs so Peggy could receive the type of coaching needed by an international star. Albert Fleming worked overtime at a local newspaper to pay for the lessons and his wife Doris, made all of their daughter's costumes. Both Carlo Fassi, a former European champion, and Dick Button, former American Olympic champion, worked with Peggy. She was soon at the top of world-class form.

Fleming won the United States championship in 1966, 1967, 1968, to give her five, consecutive titles. She won the world crown in 1966 through 1968. No one skated near her competitive edge at the time she retired. Peggy went out like a champion, winning her last world title. She built up such a commanding lead in the compulsories, which constituted 60 percent of the score, that she could win "knitting in a chair" as one writer described it. But Peggy performed her complete, spectacular program. Dressed in salmon pink, she interpreted Tchaikovsky's "Sixth Symphony" with flawless precision. At the finish the crowd roared, and the judges responded with a string of 5.9s, with two 5.8s and two perfect 6.0s. The champion took her bows.

Retirement was forced by the death of Albert Fleming in 1966. With three other children to bring up, it was financially impossible for Doris Fleming to finance her daughter's amateur career. Fleming soon became the most widely-known professional skater since Sonja Henie. She starred in a 1968 NBC television special, "Here's Peggy Fleming," and went on to perform in numerous Ice Follies productions. Despite a weakness for chocolate, the professional still maintains her five-foot-three, 110-pound figure.

Championships are only a small part of Peggy Fleming's contribution to figure skating. Peggy added a new dimension to the beauty of the sport. Lloyd Garrison described her triumph at the 1968 Olympics as a "victory of the ballet over the Ice Follies approach to figure skating." The judges concurred; she received the first-place vote of all nine to defeat Gabriele Seyfert of East Germany by the wide margin of 1970.5 to 1882.3.

On the ice she was beautiful, delicate, and feminine, with long dark hair, dark eyes, and total poise. According to Button, "With Peggy Fleming there's not a misplaced move. She's always in perfect position going into and out of her jumps." Button refers to her as the Audrey Hepburn of skating. The London *Times* capsulized Peggy's appeal on ice when it called her "America's shy Bambi."

Peggy married Greg Jenkins, a dermatologist, in 1971, and they have two children. She skated professionally for many years and said of her professional work, "I may not have been as good as I was at my peak, but I feel that I was more creative and expressive. I didn't have as much time to practice but I had confidence in front of a crowd." She is currently ice-skating commentator for ABC and is seen and heard regularly on television. Her commentary is as precise and revealing as was her skating.

Peggy Fleming was a poetess on ice skates. Perhaps she did not leap as high as some of the greatest skaters and she may have been a bit less athletic, but she certainly defined the word "graceful" as it pertained to skating.

Althea Gibson
"From Harlem to Forest Hills"
August 25, 1927–
Silver, South Carolina

It is a simple axiom: To play tennis or golf well, a person must be born with wealth. Young Althea Gibson never heard the axiom, and as she understood its implications she never let it slow her down.

Gibson was a tough competitor, from a tough background. Born in Silver, South Carolina, the oldest of five children, when her father's small cotton farm produced consistently poor crops he moved the family to 143rd Street, in New York's Harlem, and became a garage worker. Althea preferred the poolroom to the classroom and dropped out of school when she was 13. She got by doing a variety of odd jobs, including elevator operator, counter person, and even slaughtering and cleaning chickens. But she was big and strong, had considerable intelligence, and loved to play sports. As an inner-city kid she played both baskektball and handball well and excelled at paddle tennis, a variation of the lawn game played on city streets. A Police Athletic League instructor noticed her skill and introduced her to Fred Johnson, a tennis professional at the Cosmopolitan Tennis Club, one of the few racket clubs that allowed blacks in the front door. The tennis lessons she received turned a gangling 15-

Althea Gibson made the transition from Harlem street kid to Wimbledon champion (photo courtesy International Tennis Hall of Fame and Tennis Museum at the Newport Casino, Newport, RI).

year-old girl into a tennis player who could compete successfully in local tournaments. She also met and became good friends with boxer Sugar Ray Robinson and his wife, Edna Mae, at whose Harlem apartment she frequently stayed.

Life got a second boost when she was 19. Two successful black doctors who were tennis buffs, saw the potential in Gibson's game and gave her the opportunity of a lifetime. Dr. Herbert Eaton and his wife took the teen into their home in Lynchburg, Virginia, and saw to it that she renewed her education, which had been neglected for six years. Dr. Robert Johnson, a skilled player, tutored her in tennis. In 1949, 22-year-old Althea finished high school and earned an athletic scholarship to Florida A and M, where she played tennis and basketball. She was graduated in 1952 at 25 years old.

During her school years Althea played in the tournaments that would accept her. She first won the National Negro singles championship in 1948, a title she successfully defended nine years. Marion Motley was then starring for the Cleveland Browns, and Jackie Robinson had been in organized baseball for only one year. Chuck Cooper and Sweetwater Clifton were the two pioneering blacks in what became the National Basketball Association. But in tennis? No black would step on the sacred lawns of Forest Hills except to mow them!

That changed because Alice Marble and Sarah Palfrey, tennis stars of the 1930s, were instrumental in having Althea invited to the national championships at Forest Hills in 1950. She lost in the second round, but the door was open to all the better tournaments. The following year Gibson became the first black to compete at Wimbledon.

For a few years she was an ordinary player; winning sometimes but losing frequently. She was seriously considering retirement when the U.S. State Department provided her with an opportunity to tour Asia with three other players as a goodwill ambassador. Her game came together during the tour.

The Indian and Asiatic Women's singles title was her first. She then proceeded to win the French title as part of a string of 14, consecutive championships. She finally lost to an old nemesis, Shirley Fry, at Wimbledon but took the Wimbledon doubles title that year with partner Angela Buxton.

In 1957, Gibson was ranked the best woman tennis player in the world. She won the All-England singles title at Wimbledon and the United States national title at Forest Hills. New York welcomed home the one-time truant from Harlem with a tickertape parade. To show that the victories were no fluke, she successfully defended both titles in 1958. The Associated Press named her "Woman Athlete of the Year" in both 1957 and 1958.

Gibson was suddenly thirty, and in that era there was no prize money for winning tennis tournaments. It was time to make a living from her athletic skills. Gibson accepted a one-hundred-thousand-dollar offer from the Harlem Globetrotters to perform tennis exhibitions during half-time intermissions at their games. Thus she became a professional ineligible to compete in amateur tournaments. She later joined the Ladies Professional Golfing Association circuit and, although never a star, made a living from the sport. Like many golfers, she hit the ball far but not always straight.

There was life after competition. She has been a teaching tennis professional, athletic commissioner for the State of New Jersey, and a manager for the Department of Human Services. In 1971 she was elected to the Tennis Hall of Fame. She appeared in a film, "The Horse Soldiers," with John Wayne and wrote an autobiography.

Today Gibson is a manager for the Department of Recreation for the city of East Orange, New Jersey, where she is a folk hero and competes as an amateur in golf. Her primary aim is to interest poor kids in tennis. From Harlem to Forest Hills may be a short ride on the subway, but Althea Gibson was the first person to make the trip with a tennis racket under her arm.

Steffi Graf
"The Golden Grand Slammer"
June 14, 1969–
Manheim, West Germany

One trend is consistent in women's tennis; in each era one woman dominates the game for a period of years, only to be eclipsed by a new "Tennis Queen." The first international star, Suzanne Lenglen, gave way to Helen Wills, who was succeeded by Helen Jacobs. The baton has been passed from the past to the present by such stars as Alice Marble, Maureen Connolly, Margaret Smith Court, Billy Jean King, Chris Evert, and Martina Navratilova. At this writing Steffi Graf stands on this lofty pedestal.

Steffi Graf is the older of two children born to Peter and Heidi Graf in Mannheim, West Germany. Tennis was virtually the only activity Steffi has known since she was a small child. Both parents were fine players, and she received her first racket when she was four years old. Her father sold his share in an automobile dealership that he partly owed and moved the family to Bruhl, West Germany, to open a tennis school when she was young. Steffi was his prize pupil and Peter is still her coach, business manager, and, some say, a driving father.

Young Steffi was a tennis-playing sensation as a child as she breezed through tournaments in West Germany and around Europe. She was the age-group European tennis champion at 12, and at 13 she ranked twelfth among all West German women players. Steffi became a professional in 1983 while she was still 13.

It took a while to get going in the professional ranks, but once her game matured, she became invincible. Although she had no victories in 1984, her first year on the professional tour, she reached the semifinals at Wimbledon and won a gold medal at the Olympics, where tennis was played as a demonstration sport. She ranked twenty-second in the world at year's end.

Six tournament titles came in 1985, the year she turned 16, and she continued to show promise in the grand slam events. She got to round 16 at the French Open and Wimbledon, and was defeated by Navratilova in the semifinals at the United States Open. Graf won her first grand slam event, the French Open, in 1986, a year in which she won 8 of the 14 tournaments she entered.

Steffi shrewdly limited her appearances to reduce wear and tear on her body and to help focus her concentration on the tournaments in which she played. Her opponents came to shudder when she took time off from competition. She always returned with a new weapon in her arsenal. By the end of the 1986 season she was almost the complete player.

Number-one ranking in women's tennis was accorded her during the summer of 1987, a season in which she won 11 of 13 tournaments and 75 of the 77 matches she played. Her two losses were to Navratilova at Wimbledon and the United States Open. She was so consistent that season that she won 150 of the 166 sets she played. The stage was set for 1988.

In 1988, Steffi Graf became the third woman and fifth person to win the grand slam of tennis: the Australian, French, British, and United States Open championships. Don Budge was the first to collect all four titles in 1938, Rod Laver did it twice, and women Maureen Connolly in 1953 and Margaret Smith Court in 1970 had managed the feat. Only five other women have won all four events in their career; Navratilova won them consecutively, but not in the same year, Doris Hart, King, Evert, and Shirley Fry. Graf's grand slam may be the most impressive, since she accomplished it on four different surfaces against outstanding competition. She won the first leg in January at Australia on a rubberized hardcourt surface. She defeated Evert in the finals, 6–1, 7–6. Gabriela Sabatina of Argentina provided competition in the semifinals of the French Open on slow red clay, but Sabatina went down 6–3, 7–6. She had previously defeated Graf twice in 1988 in Virginia Slims competition. Steffi wiped out Natalasi Zverera of the Soviet Union in the final round, 6–0, 6–0, in less than an hour.

Steffi Graf prepares mentally to return a serve (photo courtesy Carol L. Newsom Associates/Virginia Slims).

The British Open Championship is the major tennis event of each season, and in 1988 Graf faced Navratilova in the finals on Wimbledon's fast, revered, grass courts. Navratilova had handed Graf her only defeats the previous year and was the British Open singles champion from 1982 through 1987. She also held the title consecutively in 1978 and 1979. This time it was the West German's turn, 5–7, 6–2, 6–1. After three grand slam tournaments and 21, straight grand slam singles matches, could the 19-year-old handle the pressure at the United States Open on the hard surface at Louis Armstrong Stadium in Flushing, New York? Upsets in the preliminary round made the slam easier. Zina Garrison ousted Navratilova in the quarterfinals and Evert was forced to default to Graf in the semifinals because of acute gastroenteritis. But the final opponent was on old nemesis, Gabriela Sabatini, who pushed Graf to the limit. The first set was easy, 6–3, but Sabatini was in top form in the second and trounced Steffi, 6–3. Graf put it all together in the third set and won, 6–1, for the match, championship, and grand slam. This grand slam was unique in the history of the sport because she also won the gold medal at the 1988 Summer Olympics. It was dubbed a "golden grand slam."

During 1989 she lost only two of nearly eighty matches. Arantxa Sanchez upset her in the finals of the French Open, breaking the grand slam streak and Sabatina nipped her in the finals of the Bausch and Lomb Championships.

In 1990 analyst George Lott, writing in *World Tennis*, gave this scouting report: Graf possessed (1) a great, great forehand; (2) a better-than-average serve; (3) an average backhand; (4) fine side-to-side court coverage; (5) a fair volley; (6) a perchant to go corner to corner; (7) a tall, free swing; (8) a never-say-die attitude.

People find the person Steffi Graf hard to know. On the court she is a machine, a perfect tennis player. Off the court, her associates on the circuit say, she is either very shy or extremely aloof. This should surprise no one. Steffi is only 21 as of this writing and has been exposed to little except dad and tennis. She also was under extreme pressure during the 1990 season, when her father received much adverse press in the European scandal sheets. During the next few years she will have a chance to blossom into her own self. Her game is so complete that experts feel she will dominate women's tennis into the next century. Her chances are good, because among her chief rivals Evert has retired and Navratilova is 12 years older than she. Graf has the potential to be an all-time great in women's tennis.

How good is Graf? In a recent radio interview with Bill Mazur, Don Budge, who has great knowledge of the game, stated that he believes Graf could have beaten Suzanne Lenglen and Helen Wills in their prime. "Yes," he suggested, "I think she is the best woman to ever play the game."

There is, however, always another challenger coming along. Monica Seles of Yugoslavia, rated third in the world, defeated Graf 6–4, 6–3, in the finals of the 1990 German Open, breaking a 60-match streak, and Jennifer Capriati, six years Graf's junior, looks like she may be a dominant factor within a few years. Time will tell.

Delorez Florence Griffith-Joyner

"FloJo"
December 21, 1959–
Los Angeles, California

She exploded off the starting blocks with acceleration never before seen in women's track. At 50 meters, the halfway point, the contest was over. "Flo-Jo" flashed her victory smile and glided home comfortably ahead of the field. Florence Griffith-Joyner had won the 1988 Olympic 100-meter dash to establish herself as the "World's Fastest Woman." Three months before she had never won a 100-meter dash in world-class competition.

Griffith-Joyner was at the top of the track world only from July through September 1988, but it was a spectacular three months. She began by qualifying for the United States Olympic team with an unprecedented, record-setting effort and subsequently gathered three golds and a silver medal at the Seoul Olympics. These amazing sprinting feats had to share equal billing with a flamboyant style, knack for dressing, and charisma.

Florence Griffith came from a large family and grew up in the Watts section of Los Angeles. She was the seventh of 11 children and was raised by her mother. Her parents divorced when she was four. Florence's mother worked hard as a seamstress and did a fine job providing for the family. "I had a very happy childhood," she says, "There were never days when we did not have food. . . . We didn't know how poor we were; we were rich as family." She feels that her brothers and sisters all grew up to be good people because "we were afraid of Mama's voice."

At 11 she was running in meets sponsored by the Sugar Ray Robinson Youth Foundation. She moved up to the Jesse Owens National Youth Games as a 14-year-old and consistently won every dash she entered. A star in the long jump and sprints at Jordan High School in Los Angeles, she entered California State University at Northridge to study business. There Coach Bob Kersee convinced her that she had the potential to be an outstanding athlete. Kersee accepted a coaching position at UCLA, and she transferred, for he is considered to be the most technically competent among women's track coaches. With his training and her natural speed she was good enough to finish fourth in the 200-meters run at the United States Olympic qualifying meet in 1980 when she was 20.

Florence was a consistent runner but never really considered to be "world class" throughout most of her career. She won the National Collegiate Athletic

Florence Griffith-Joyner, the sprinting star of the 1988 summer Olympics (photo courtesy UCLA).

Association (NCAA) 400-meter title in 1983 and finished second at 200 meters. She was never particularly effective at 100 meters because she was relatively slow coming off the starting blocks. Florence established her reputation as both a world-class runner and a flashy dresser when she won the silver medal at 200 meters during the 1984 Olympics in her home town, Los Angeles. Although she was soundly defeated by Valarie Briscoe, an old high school rival, in the finals, Griffith stole the show with her red-white-and-blue-painted, six-inch fingernails.

Disappointed with her second-place finish in the Olympics, she dropped out of serious competition and went to work as a bank representative during the day and a beautician at night. She slacked off in her training and put on weight. She appeared to be a "has-been" in track.

Then in 1987 she resumed training with the aim of winning a gold medal at the 1988 Olympics. She slimmed down to a svelte but powerful 130 pounds. That year she also married Al Joyner and worked with her athlete husband and Bob Kersee to develop explosiveness in her start. The relationships of the three are frequently confused: Bob Kersee is the husband of Jackie Joyner-Kersee, the pentathlete; Al Joyner, Florence's husband, is Joyner-Kersee's brother.

Griffith-Joyner concentrated on leg-strengthening exercises on weight-lifting machines and ran longer distances to develop stamina. After more than a year on this regimen her thighs were as powerful as those of many athletic men. She changed jobs so that she worked only four hours a day in employee relations for the Anheuser-Busch Brewing Company. She was ready for the Olympic trials held in July of 1988.

Griffith-Joyner ran a 10.49 in the second heat of the 100-meter dash, smashing the existing world record of 10.76 by more than a quarter of a second. In her four 100-meter runs at the trials, she beat the existing world record four times. She easily won the finals at 100 meters and followed that up with a 200-meter run that established a new American record. She became a pre–Olympic favorite to win both dashes.

At the Olympics FloJo ran 10.54 in the 100 meters, a new Olympic record and close to her sensational world-record time. She broke the existing world record twice in the 200-meter run. She added a third gold medal to her collection when she ran the third leg on the 4-by-100-meter relay team and completed her performance with a silver medal in the 4-by-400-meter relay.

Retired from competition in February of 1989, she has a successful career as model, actress, and product endorser. Florence Griffith-Joyner is certainly the most glamorous woman track athlete to catch the public's eye in several decades.

Dorothy Hamill

"Overcoming the Jitters"
March 12, 1956–
Riverside, Connecticut

Dorothy Hamill did not figure to be a great figure skater. She started relatively late, and her parents had little interest in skating. Riverside, Connecticut, a section of Greenwich, about 45 minutes by commuter train from midtown New York, is not known for developing world-class skaters.

It all started when Dorothy received a pair of ice skates as a present one Christmas when she was about eight years old and tried them out at a nearby frozen pond. She soon taught herself to skate but was frustrated because she could not skate backwards. Dorothy asked her father if she could attend group skating lessons at a nearby rink. She made herself into the top woman figure skater in the world with eleven years of dedication.

Dorothy slowly progressed when compared with other stars. She became the best local skater but was unknown nationally. Dorothy dropped out of school when she was 14 to devote fulltime to skating, earning her high school diploma through private tutoring. Although she trained for eight hours a day, six days per week, 11 months per year, she lacked the one ingredient she needed to become an international star—top-rate coaching. Her father footing the bills, she moved to Colorado to work with Carlo Fassi, Peggy Fleming's coach.

North Americans have excelled in international figure-skating competition. Although Norwegian Sonja Henie dominated the sport until World War II, post-war Olympic champions included Canadian Barbara Ann Scott in 1948, and Americans Tenley Albright in 1956, Carol Heiss in 1960, and Peggy Fleming in 1968. Austrian Trixi Shuba won the gold in 1972 with Canadian Karen Magnussen second followed by Americans Janet Lynn and Julie Holmes. Hamill, who was 15 at the time, could not yet compete with these great skaters.

Only two women held the United States figure skating championship during the ten-year period from 1964 through 1973, Peggy Fleming for the first five years and Janet Lynn for the next five. But in 1974, the 17-year-old Hamill was ready to emerge. Lynn left amateur competition after winning the 1973 United States title, clearing the path for runner-up Dorothy Hamill to take over as the finest American women's figure skater. She won her first United States championship at Providence, Rhode Island, in February 1974 and

Dorothy Hamill shows the perfect form that made her a champion (photo courtesy World Figure Skating Museum).

repeated in 1975 and 1976. Hamill also was approaching the top on the international scene. She finished second to East Germany's Christine Errath for the world crown in 1974, and was runner-up to Dianne de Leeuw, a Los Angeles resident who represented the Netherlands, in 1975.

Stage fright was the one huge barrier. Just before she began her free-skating program at the 1975 World Championships, Dorothy mistook a round of boos intended for the scores of the previous skater as being directed at her. She left the ice in tears, returning to skate brilliantly when informed of what really happened. Her nervousness often forced her into conservative free skating, and critics noticed that she frequently omitted difficult maneuvers when she knew that she was in the lead. This would have to stop if she were to be a champion at the 1976 Olympic games.

Hamill easily won the 1976 United States championship on her way to the

Olympic competition, but two former world champions, Dianne de Leeuw and Christine Errath, and two future world champions, Anett Potzsch of East Germany and Linda Fratianne of the United States, were waiting for her at Innsbruck. She would have to be at her best.

Preparation for the Olympics was meticulous. Coach Fassi worked on her confidence and technical skating; and Brian Foley polished her choreography. Her father chose the music she would dance to. He made an unusual selection, the background music from old Errol Flynn movies.

Olympic scoring consisted of 30 percent for compulsory figures, 20 percent for the short program, and 50 percent for free skating. Dorothy was near the top of the pack after the compulsories, and, most important, ahead of her principle rivals. Hamill's two-minute short program delighted the audience and judges. Fred Tupper of the *New York Times* reported: "Miss Hamill. . .the best spinner in free-skating. . .leaped into a delayed axel, then a double axel and in succession executed a flying sitspin, a double flip, then a double toe loop. The audience was all hers now, and she wound up with dazzling stepwork and a layback spin." The performance produced a row of 5.9s and 5.8s, with one rare 6.0 for technical merit. Hamill was in the lead.

In the free skating program the next day she executed flawlessly and had the crowd in the palm of her hand. She concluded her performance with her trademark, the "Hamill Camel" (a camel spin into a sitspin with a spin coming out), that brought the house down. Dorothy was rated first by all nine judges. Three young girls were needed to help her pick up the flowers that the fans rained down on her. She had beaten her opponents and the jitters.

Although it was anticlimactic, Dorothy won her only world championship a few weeks later in Sweden. With no more worlds to conquer in amateur skating, it was time to move on to a professional career. Contracts with the ABC network and the Ice Capades in 1977 made her the highest paid woman athlete of her era, over $2 million dollars in her first two years as a professional. She is still a hot item in the advertising business as a spokesperson for Bausch and Lomb who is seen frequently in their contact lens advertising campaigns. She still projects a totally wholesome image that appeals to both men and women.

Hamill entered figure skating just as Peggy Fleming was redefining poetic grace. Dorothy was athletic. Peggy danced and interpreted divinely. Dorothy leaped, spun and performed at great speed, yet had a wonderful feel for the music to which she skated. Both were great; each was her own person. The sport of figure skating is richer because of them.

Carol Elizabeth Heiss

"Intestinal Fortitude"
January 20, 1940–
Queens, New York

Too many have forgotten how great a champion Carol Heiss was. Dick Button rates Sonja Henie first among the all-time women greats, and lists Peggy Fleming and Katarina Witt somewhere behind her. His opinions are solid and well-respected, but Carol Heiss could compete with any of them.

Heiss was 16 years old in 1956, the first year she won the world figure skating championship. She held that title through 1960. She also won the United States figure skating championship four years consecutively, from 1957 through 1960, and was the Olympic champion in 1960.

There is more to this skater than figures on ice. Carol grew up in the Ozone Park section of Queens, her parents were Germans who emigrated to the United States during the 1920s. Her father was a baker; her mother designed textiles, and both were from the old school that believed it was their life's work to make things better for their children. They sacrificed much for their family of two girls and a boy.

Like many city kids, Carol's first skates had wheels on them and she progressed to ice skates when she was five. By the time she was seven, Carol was making the daily subway trip to Manhattan for five hours of practice at the rink atop of old Madison Square Garden under the tutelage of Pierre Brunet, who, with his wife, won the Olympic pair-skating championship for France in 1928 and 1932. At eleven Heiss was the national novice champion; at 12 she won the national junior title. She was on her way to world recognition when a freak accident almost ended her career at the age of 14. Her left leg was badly slashed when she accidently bumped into her sister during a practice session. Her sister's blade severed a tendon in her lower leg, and for months it was uncertain whether she would skate again. But her family encouraged her, and by the following winter she was skating competitively.

Tenley Albright was the reigning figure-skating queen during the mid–1950s. Albright won the United States championship from 1952 through 1956 and was the 1955 world champion. But young Carol Heiss was closing in, finishing second to Albright in the 1955 World, North American, and United States championships. Heiss was ready to challenge the champion in 1956.

Albright clearly beat Heiss for the 1956 Olympic title; she was placed first by 10 of the 11 judges, although the actual point score, 169.69 to 168.02,

Carol Heiss, the schoolgirl from Queens, NY, who became a skating queen (photo courtesy World Figure Skating Museum).

looked closer. Heiss was tired of being runner-up to Albright, though, and two weeks later turned the tables on her, winning the world title, her first of five, consecutive championships. Heiss was just past her sixteenth birthday; only Sonja Henie, at 15, was younger. From that point until she retired after the 1960 Olympics Carol Heiss was never outscored.

Her mother died in 1956 when Carol was 16, so, in addition to her school work and skating practice, she cooked the meals at home and helped raise her younger brother and sister. Both siblings became outstanding figure skaters. Nancy Heiss finished second to Carol in the 1959 United States national competition, and Bruce Heiss won many men's titles. Carol was also a fine student and won a full scholarship to prestigious New York University where she earned a bachelor of arts degree while competing internationally.

On April 30, 1960, Carol married David Jenkins, a three-time world figure-skating champion who won the United States men's title the four years that Carol won the women's championship. Like Carol he was the 1960 Olympic champion.

Heiss-Jenkins was a professional for a short time and even appeared in a movie, "Snow White and the Three Stooges," but retired happily to family life in Akron, Ohio, with her husband and three children (who all skate well). She returned to the sport in recent years as an instructor who is as devoted to her pupils as she was to her own development when she was a youngster. She regularly spends 12 hours a day coaching potential champions and evaluating their progress with David, her equally-skilled husband. When asked what the Olympic gold medal meant to her, Carol, a product of the 1950s, said, "The gold medal doesn't wash the kitchen floor, and it doesn't change the children's diapers." With the remuneration associated with winning today, it would, but perhaps today we do not produce champions with her intestinal fortitude.

Joan Joyce
"The 116-mile-per-hour Pitcher"
August 1, 1940–
Waterbury, Connecticut

Nolan Ryan is one of the most talked about phenomena in the history of sports, partly because he threw a fastball over 90 miles per hour when in his forties. Ninety miles per hour is the barrier that distinguishes truly fast major league pitchers from merely quick ones. One occasionally hears a report of a pitcher being clocked at 100 miles per hour. Most players conclude that they would not like to bat against him. As scary as it might be to see a delivery of 90 miles per hour from 60 feet, consider a 116-mile-per-hour pitch thrown from only 45 feet. That is what softball players faced when Joan Joyce was on the mound.

Joan Joyce, the finest women's softball player of all time (photo courtesy Amateur Softball Association, Oklahoma City, Oklahoma).

Joyce grew up in a family that worked and played hard. Her father was an active baseball coach in the Waterbury, Connecticut, area and Joan was around ballfields from the time she could walk. Although an outstanding baseball player as a youngster, it was not her favorite sport. She preferred basketball and played it well. She also excelled in volleyball, learned the basics of golf, and had a bowling average of 180 as a teenager. But softball was the game that would make her famous.

Joan started playing for the Raybestos Brakettes, one of the best women's softball teams in the country, during summer school break when she was 14. The Brakettes were so highly rated because Bertha Tickey, their pitcher, had a 757–88 record in her 20-year career. When Joan joined the team, Bertha was a grandmother in her forties and approaching the end of her career. Joan took over the primary pitching duties when she was 17 in 1957, and compiled the finest statistics in the history of women's softball.

Joyce was an Amateur Softball Association All-American from 1957 through 1975. The 19-year streak would have continued except that she became a professional in 1976. The Brakettes won 12 national titles behind Joan's pitching. She also pitched for the Orange, California, Lionettes for three seasons and led them to a national title in 1965. During her three years in California she played Amateur Athletic Union (AAU) basketball, was a member of the national team, and was a three-time All-American basketball player.

It is difficult to point to one "best" softball playoff performance, but 1973 would be a candidate. She pitched and won all nine games for the Raybestos Brakettes at the Women's National Fast Pitch Championship that year, had eight shutouts and hit .414. In 1975 she was undefeated on the mound, completing a 36–0 record, her fourth perfect season. She was selected as the Most Valuable Player at the national playoffs for the eighth time.

Her career statistics as an amateur softball player are astonishing. She won 507 games while losing only 33 for a .940 winning percentage. That included 105 no-hitters, 33 perfect games, and a lifetime 0.21 earned run average. Her lifetime batting average was .327.

After a brief stay at New York's Brooklyn College as its softball coach, Joan became one of the driving forces behind establishing women's professional softball. Joan owned, managed, and played on the Connecticut Falcons of the Women's Professional Softball League from 1976 through 1979. She was also the league's commissioner.

The Falcons won the Women's Pro World Series in each of the four years she was at the helm. Her playing contributed; she compiled a 101–15 pitching record, threw 34 no-hitters, and had eight perfect games. Joan's batting average was the only sign that she was slowing down now that she was in her late 30s. She hit a mere .290.

Never one to rest on her laurels, Joan polished her golf game in the mid–1970s and qualified for the Ladies Professional Golf Association (LPGA) tour in 1977. Joan is a consistent tour player although never a big winner. She is also a teaching professional at Deer Creek Country Club in Florida.

Joan's achievements have been recognized. She was inducted into the National Softball Hall of Fame in 1983 and the Women's Sports Foundation Hall of Fame the following year. She is an all-time great.

Billy Jean Moffitt King
"B.J."
November 22, 1943–
Long Beach, California

There have been better women athletes than Billy Jean King. Babe Didrikson and Jackie Joyner-Kersee were surely more versatile. Most experts consider Helen Wills, Suzanne Lenglen, Steffi Graf, and Martina Navratilova better tennis players. But King may be the most important woman athlete of all time.

Billy Jean Moffitt, known as "B.J." to her friends, grew up in Long Beach, California. Although her father had been an athlete in college, neither he nor his wife ever played tennis. Billy Jean was a fine baseball player as a youngster, but she was only the second-best ballplayer in the family. Her brother, Randy, had a career as a relief pitcher for the San Francisco Giants during the 1970s. Billy Jean took some tennis lessons at a local playground when she was eleven and fell in love with the game.

B.J. improved steadily as a teenager, and by 1960 when she was a junior in high school, ranked nineteenth nationally. During her senior year she lived weekends with Alice Marble, the tennis champion from the 1930s, who coached her free-of-charge. Within a year, Moffitt's national ranking improved to fourth.

Moffitt's name first appeared in the headlines in 1962 when, as an unseeded player, she defeated Margaret Smith Court, the reigning tennis queen, in first-round play at Wimbledon. Devastated by Smith Court, 6–1, in the 18-minute first set, Moffitt showed her character by rallying to win the next two sets, 6–3, 7–5. Although she was later eliminated in the quarterfinal round, Billy Jean did win the Wimbledon doubles title in 1962 for the second year in a row.

One of Wimbledon's great champions, she won All-England championships, a mark yet to be topped. She won six singles titles, three consecutively from 1966 through 1968, and in 1972, 1973, and 1975, and she was a finalist on three other occasions. She also won ten doubles and four mixed-doubles championships.

She won the United States title at Forest Hills four times and one other national championship in each year from 1966 through 1972, as shown in the following listing of her peak period triumphs.

Year	British	United States	Other National Championships
1966	won		South Africa
1967	won	won	South Africa
1968	won	finalist	Australia
1969	finalist		South Africa
1970	finalist		Italy
1971		won	West Germany
1972	won	won	France
1973	won		
1974		won	
1975	won		

Billy Jean competed as an amateur through 1967, and in the spring of 1968 became a professional. She married a college friend, Larry King, who was a lawyer and managed her career. King began a long and successful crusade to have the purses in women's tournaments equal to the men's. A typical tournament win in the late 1960s earned a man $10,000, a woman $2,000. Within a few years, an aging tennis hustler would provide the opportunity to demonstrate that women's tennis was a marketable commodity.

September 20, 1973, was the finest day of Billy Jean's tennis career. Her triumph was not at the lawns of Forest Hills nor the courts of Wimbledon, but in the spacious Houston Astrodome; her opponent, a 55-year-old tennis player turned promoter, Bobby Riggs.

Riggs had loudly proclaimed for years that women did not deserve an equal share of tournament tennis purses because they did not play as well as men. To prove his point, Riggs played a series of bizarre tennis exhibitions, sometimes playing in women's outfits, complete with high heels. He generally won these matches because he was a decent tennis player and accustomed to the limelight. He won the United States singles championship in 1939 and 1941

Billy Jean King, probably the most important woman athlete ever (photo courtesy Carol B. Newsom Associates/Virginia Slims).

and was runner-up in 1940, the year he won at Wimbledon. He overwhelmed the great Margaret Smith Court, 6–2, 6–1, in a 1973 Mother's Day match when he caught that champion totally unprepared mentally for the circus environment. The stage was set for the one-hundred-thousand-dollar Battle of the Sexes, "The Libber," 29-year-old Billy Jean King, versus the "Lobber," Bobby Riggs, self-styled "male chauvinist pig." More than 30,000 attended in person and 40 million watched on a 37-nation television hookup. Billy Jean devoured Bobby in straight sets, 6–4, 6–3, 6–3. After the match, Billy Jean shouted for joy, "I feel this is the culmination of 19 years of tennis for me." She later confided, "I was amazed at how weak an opponent he was."

It was not easy for Billy Jean to become a star. She is relatively short and chunky, standing five feet, four and one-half inches and weighing between 130 and 140 pounds. She always had to fight an expanding waistline during the off-season. Her 20/400 vision is hardly the primary prerequisite for a great athlete. And for a woman who is so outspoken and forceful, she was shy as a youngster; she would be speechless in school when required to make a report in front of her class.

After the Riggs match, Billy Jean became the personification of women's tennis. She was instrumental in establishing both the World Team Tennis League and the Virginia Slims touring circuit for women. Between 1970 and 1977 she won 29 Virginia Slims singles titles and was a World Team Tennis All-Star three times. As late as 1980, when she was 36 and suffering from severe knee problems, she teamed with Navratilova to win the United States Women's Doubles title. She retired from tennis competition in 1981.

Billy Jean King earned much acclaim. The Associated Press named her "Woman Athlete of the Year" in 1967 and 1973. *Sports Illustrated* named her "Sportsperson of the Year" in 1972 and she was *Time* "Woman of the Year" in 1976. *Harper's Bazaar* listed her among the "10 Most Powerful Women in America" in 1977.

Today many women tennis players make six-figure annual incomes in purses and endorsements. These players should pause regularly to remember the person who, more than anyone else, put the extra zeroes at the end of their paychecks.

Julie Krone

"Julie Does"
July 24, 1963–
Benton Harbor, Michigan

The New York tabloids ran an advertisement during the fall of 1989 that read:

WHO WINS AT THE MEADOWLANDS MORE THAN
THE GIANTS, JETS, DEVILS AND NETS COMBINED?
JULIE DOES

"Julie" is Julie Krone, the most adept woman jockey ever to ride a thoroughbred.

At the time of the ad, Krone had climbed aboard 205 mounts for the fall Meadowlands meet, won 58 races, and finished in the money 113 times. Her horses had won 28 percent of their races and finished in the money 59 percent of the time. The numbers were nothing new. Julie won the Meadowlands track riding title in 1987 and 1988, so adding the 1989 crown was routine. She is the most successful of all the jockeys who compete at the New Jersey and Pennsylvania tracks.

Horse racing is one of the few sports where women and men compete equally. The jockey must control a 1200-pound animal that runs nearly 40 miles per hour. Fortunately, the animal is intelligent and sensitive, and responds well to a person who knows how to coax a top performance. Krone is a gifted and sensitive rider. The people who work around the barns at the Eastern tracks say, "Horses run well for her."

Julie grew up loving horses. Dad taught art at Benton Harbor High School in Eau Claire, Michigan, and moonlighted at Lake Michigan College. Mom bred and showed Arabian horses. Julie's parents separated when she was a teenager; dad continued teaching, and mom tended bar and encouraged her daughter to excel in horses. At age three she rode a horse for a half mile with no assistance and showed Arabians when she was a child. She became a skilled dressage rider and started racing horses at county fairs. The summer before her 16th birthday, Julie's mother made a slight alteration on her birth certificate, changing the month of birth from July to April, so that she could get a job at Churchill Downs working around the stables and walking sweaty horses. Julie was in her environment. But to the people who hire jockeys Julie was "a cute little girl from a small town in Michigan" who was a decent rider. Her attitude has always been, "If you want a girl jockey, get someone else." She felt she could ride with the best of them.

The State of Maryland issued the first jockey's license to a woman, Kathy Kusner, in 1968. Several women have done well in the sport, notably Robyn Smith, who later married Fred Astaire. Actually, about 25 percent of the licensed jockeys today are women but they seldom ride for the big stakes at the famous tracks. They are "woman jockeys." Julie Krone is a jockey.

The essence of recognition is when the world knows a person by first name. Ringo, Winston, Ella, Martina, or Elton. Around the race tracks there are three jockeys with universally-recognized names: Willie, Angel, and Julie.

Julie Krone, the greatest female rider in racing history (photo courtesy New York Racing Association).

Julie worked her way up through the tracks of Maryland, Pennsylvania, and New Jersey to the big-time metropolitan New York circuit, but in racetrack parlance, it was a rough trip. She was rightfully nailed for a 60-day suspension at Bowie racetrack in Maryland as a 17-year-old when a routine search turned up marijuana in her car. She learned her lesson: "I can blame youth and stupidity. It cured me of doing dope. It made me very conscious of my image."

The same year she fell from a mount at Laurel Park and was out for four months with a broken back. When she returned her rhythm was not there. Krone mounted 80 consecutive horses without a winner. She heard the talk. Just another "girl jockey." She had to show them.

Julie had the most wins at the Atlantic City meets in both 1982 and 1983, not exactly the big time, but beating the best male jockeys in the area. By 1986 she was riding at Monmouth and winning as many as any jockey on the East Coast. One day she brought home six winners, and a week later had four on a card in New York. A few of the male jockeys resented her success and put her to the test.

One day at Monmouth, jockey Miguel Rujana slashed Krone across the face with his whip as their horses battled down the stretch. The blow drew blood from Julie's ear. At the post-race weigh-in, Julie punched Miguel in the nose. Miguel then shoved Julie into a nearby pool. Dripping wet, she got out and conked Miguel with a chair. Both riders were set down to think about their indiscretions, but the word was out, "Tangle with Julie if you choose, but she'll fight back."

Julie was hassled several more times, but as Angel Cordero, her friend and mentor, says, "The only way you stop that is just winning." Julie did.

With two feet planted on the ground, Julie is a tomboy and a tease. Astride a horse she is reckless and aggressive. Her squeaky voice, described as sounding like a chipmonk's, belies her toughness. She is one of three American jockeys to win six races on one afternoon. In 1987, when she was 24, she won 364 races, the sixth best in the country, and won riding titles at Monmouth and the Meadowlands. She successfully defended both titles in 1988 and 1989. That year, 1987, she won her one thousandth race and earned the respect of her fellow riders. During the 1980s Julie won nearly 17 percent of her races, with 1899 victories on 11,433 mounts. She earned $27.67 million in purses for the owner who let her ride. By 1988, she was the fourth leading jockey in the United States and in 1989 was rated third.

She finished the 1989 season in typical Krone fashion. She fell from a horse in the Meadowlands on November 24 severely breaking her arm. While she recuperated, she served a 15-day suspension for a fight with a fellow jockey in September.

Andrea Mead Lawrence

"Andy"
April 19, 1932–
Rutland, Vermont

On those occasions when Andrea Mead Lawrence fell, which alpine skiers do frequently, she got herself up and battled her way to the finish line. Her career and life have had ups and downs, but, regardless of the circumstances, Lawrence always came back fighting.

Andrea Mead was on skis before she was four. Her parents managed a small resort at Pico Peak, Vermont, so it was natural for her to be on the slopes all day during the long New England winters. Carl Acker, a fine ski instructor from Switzerland, worked at the resort, and so top-level coaching was readily available.

Serious competition began when she was 11 and she qualified for the 1948 U.S. Olympic team at age 14, winning the trials in the slalom. The 1948 Winter Olympic Games, the first held in 12 years because of World War II, were conducted in St. Moritz, Switzerland. She was not ready for world competition at that stage of her career and finished thirty-fifth in the downhill event, twenty-first in the combined alpine (the event that evolved into the giant slalom) and eighth in the slalom. Gretchen Fraser was the star of the American team, winning a gold medal in the slalom and a silver in the combined. But "Andy" returned to the States a confident and seasoned competitor and soon established herself as the finest alpine skier in the nation.

Mead won the downhill, combined, and slalom in the United States national competition in 1950. In 1951 she concentrated on the international ski circuit, representing the United States, and in 16 events, won ten and placed second four times. Andrea married David Lawrence, also a world-class skier, in Davos, Switzerland, in 1951 and competed thereafter as Andrea Mead Lawrence.

She entered the 1952 Olympics at Oslo with the pressure of being one of the favorites. The giant slalom, was the first Olympic event; she won it convincingly, beating her nearest competitor by 2.2 seconds. The margin was spectacular because the course had been shortened due to poor snow conditions, so bad that Norwegian soldiers had to shovel snow throughout the previous night to prepare the course for the following day's skiing.

She showed what she was made of in the slalom, six days after her giant

Andrea Mead Lawrence, America's finest women's Alpine skier (photo courtesy *Ski Racing* magazine).

slalom victory. The slalom requires two runs over a zigzagging course. The Associated Press described her first run this way:

> Racing down the 508-yard slope today at blinding speed, Mrs. Lawrence tried to make a difficult right turn at one of the 49 control gates near the top of the hill. She skidded and went spinning into the soft snow while the crowd of 15,000 lining the hillside groaned. . . . The United States star quickly got up

and continued the run with a wild recklessness that brought cheers from the spectators.

Other accounts mention that she caught the tip of her ski on a gate and, after falling, had to gain a few yards back up the hill to go through the gate and complete the course. Her scrambling left her in fourth place with one run to go. Her second run blew away the competition, giving a combined time of 2:10.6 to runner-up Ossi Reichart's 2:11.2. "I knew I had to do it so I just cut loose," the 19-year-old girl remarked.

Andrea began raising a family after the 1952 games. She had three children before the 1956 games convened in Cortina, Italy. Andrea competed that year but was not a factor, although she had one fourth-place finish. In 1960, when husband David Lawrence was the U.S. ski team coach and Andrea the manager, she had the honor of skiing with the Olympic torch to light the Olympic flame in Squaw Valley.

Andrea went through a bleak period in her life after her successful skiing career. When she was 35 years old in 1967, she and David divorced, and she was left to raise her five children on her own. Struggling to support the family, she got by giving skiing lessons at several resorts in the Mammouth Lakes region of California. Somehow she found time for community projects and became one of the leading environmentalists in the area. When her children were raised, the 50-year-old ran for public office and was elected a county supervisor, an office she holds at this time.

"I'm a product of Vermont and that old Yankee tradition of community service," she recently said. She also found time to write a book, *A Practice of Mountains*, a thoughtful, often poetic account of her love for skiing and mountain climbing.

Mead Lawrence competed in another era, and readily admits she skied primarily for the fun of it. But she brought an inner toughness to the sport that was honed on the hills of Vermont. At 19 she had to get off her backside, climb up a hill and get back in the race. She did that several more times in life.

Nancy Lopez

"The other 'Super Mex'"
January 6, 1957–
Torrance, California

Ask a golf fan who "Super Mex" is and the reflex answer will be Lec Trevino, the legendary Mexican-American golfer. A pause for reflection will produce a second answer: Nancy Lopez, a response with which Trevino concurs. Also a Mexican-American, Lopez, is the best of a very good crop of current women golfers.

In 1978, as a golf rookie, Lopez broke the earnings record for first-year men or women players. She took home $190,000 that year and $215,000 the next. People immediately accepted Nancy as the best woman golfer on the tour as if she had been born to inherit the mantle. But few would have staked a nickel on her chances of reaching golfing stardom a few years before.

Nancy was born in Torrance, California, in 1957, but her family moved to Rosewell, New Mexico, when she was a young girl. They were hard-working family people who devoted their lives to their children. Domingo Lopez owned an auto body shop and did well enough to find time to be a 3-handicap golfer at the local public courses. Marina Lopez was a decent golfer who gave up the game and gave her clubs to Nancy because she felt it was important for her daughter to have a chance to play well. Marina died just when Nancy was beginning to make her mark on the professional tour. No doubt she realized, as did the golfing enthusiasts in the New Mexico area, that her daughter was on her way to stardom.

Nancy's father was her coach. He emphasized the mental rather than the physical aspects of the game. Nancy claims that she received only two important playing tips in her career, from her dad, and from Lee Trevino. Her father's philosophy: "Come up real slow, come up real high, extend real far and hit the ball right in the sweet spot, and hit it right in the middle of the fairway, and then keep hitting it until you hit it into the hole." When she asked Trevino for advice about her imperfect swing, he replied, "If you swing badly but score well and win, don't change a thing."

From these tidbits, Nancy Lopez, a natural, became a great golfing champion.

The public courses of Rosewell were her training grounds because that was all her family could afford, and Mexican-Americans were not made to feel comfortable on the area's private courses. When Nancy was 12, she won the

Nancy Lopez, a golfing hall-of-famer (photo courtesy Ladies Professional Golf Association).

women's amateur championship of New Mexico, firing a women's course-record 75 at the University South course in Albuquerque. Nancy was thrilled, not so much for the victory, but because her father bought her a Barbie doll to celebrate it. She still collects dolls.

Lopez won the United States Junior Girls and Western Junior Girls Championships in 1972, 1973, and 1974 and the Mexican Amateur in 1975. She received a golf scholarship to Tulsa University and quickly became the best amateur woman golfer in the country. She finished second in the United States Women's Open at age 17 in 1976 and added that year's National Collegiate title to her laurels. But money was scarce in the Lopez household, and, after she completed two years of college, Domingo Lopez obtained a $50,000 bank loan to finance her professional career.

Neither the men's nor women's golf tour has had another such rookie; she immediately turned the Ladies Professional Golf Association (LPGA) upside-down. She finished second in her first three appearances and then went into a temporary slump, emotionally overwhelmed by her mother's early death. Nancy, ever sensitive to family needs, has always felt that her mother's death has inspired her to try harder.

After a month's layoff, she won tournaments in February and March of 1978, lost one in sudden death, and then won an unprecedented five tournaments in a row. The streak included the LPGA championship at King Island, Ohio, won with scores of 71, 65, 69, and 70, for a total of 275. Other great woman golfers, Mickey Wright, Kathy Whitworth, and Shirley Englehorn, had run off four consecutively, but Lopez is all by herself with five. She won nine tournaments that year and was the recipient of the Vare Trophy for the lowest average on the professional tour, 71.76 strokes.

Nancy Lopez was voted "Rookie of the Year" and "Golfer of the Year" for the women's tour. The Associated Press named her "Female Athlete of the Year."

Her second year on the tour, 1979, was almost as successful. She won eight of the 19 tournaments she entered and established an LPGA stroke-per-round average of 71.20, which she improved in 1985. She was again named LPGA "Golfer of the Year."

Nancy won more than $165,000 each year that she has been on the tour since 1978, although several seasons her participation was limited because she was raising a family. In 1982 Nancy married Ray Knight, a major-league third-baseman for the Cincinnati Reds and, later, the New York Mets. They have two children, Ashley and Erinn. She was previously married to television sports-caster Tim Melton in 1979. Lopez was the first woman professional to take her children with her on tour. "I can decide to play a tournament one week and then stay home and rest. You need a nanny. Fortunately, I have the financial resources."

Nancy surpassed the million-dollar mark in tour earnings in 1983 when she was 26. She played only 12 tournaments that year because she was pregnant. She was back in top form by 1985 and won the LPGA Championship by eight strokes. Nancy won that title again in 1988. They were her third and fourth LPGA wins and all four tournaments were won at different locations. Her 1985 average of 70.73 for 93 rounds is a standard that may never be topped. She won the Henredon Classic that year with the lowest 72-hole total ever recorded on the tour, 66, 67, 69, 66, total 268. By 1989, Nancy had climbed to second place in career earnings on the LPGA tour with over $2.5 million, only $100,000 less than all-time leader Pat Bradley. Lopez became a member of the Ladies Professional Hall of Fame in 1987 when she was only 30 years old. The requirements for entry are thirty tournament titles and two victories in the major tourneys. At that time Nancy had thirty victories, three LPGA championships and one Dinah Shore Open. She was selected the LPGA "Player of the Year" for the fourth time in 1988.

Champion, mother, and all-around nice person. Nancy Lopez is a hall-of-famer in many ways.

Patricia Keller McCormick
"Double-double"
May 12, 1930–
Seal Beach, California

Olympic women's diving competition has had a long and grand tradition. Greta Johansson of Sweden won the first gold medal in platform diving in 1912 and the springboard event was added in 1920. During 80 years of competition no one has dominated women's diving as did Patricia McCormick during the 1950s.

McCormick won both the platform and springboard events in two successive Olympiads, 1952 in Helsinki and 1956 at Melbourne, four gold medals in four attempts. In the history of Olympic competition, only two other women, Dorothy Poynton Hill of the United States and Ingrid Engel-Kramer of Germany, ever successfully defended an Olympic diving championship; and only two other women, Engel-Kramer and Victoria Draves of the United States, won both titles in one Olympic year. It was not until 1988 that a man, Greg Louganis, won both titles in successive Olympic games to equal Patricia's "double-double."

The 1956 victories were remarkable because she faced training complications that Louganis never encountered; she delivered a son only five months before the Melbourne competition. She swam one-half mile a day until two days before her son was born to stay in shape during her pregnancy. A few weeks after the birth she was back at her full routine of nearly 100 dives a day, six days a week. That is a lot of ladder climbing. Her husband, Glenn, an airline pilot, was her coach.

McCormick grew up as Pat Keller in Seal Beach, California. She and her two older brothers were raised almost single-handedly by their mother, who worked fulltime as a nurse. The Keller kids spent much of their spare time at Muscle Beach, where Patricia developed an interest in physical fitness, swimming, and diving. "Muscle Beach helped me as a diver because I became physically strong," she said later. She learned to dive off a float at Alamitos Bay and, although she was self-trained, she became the best of the local divers. In 1947, when she was 16, she was spotted diving at a local meet by the coach of the Los Angeles Athletic Club who invited her to work out with the fine swimmers and divers who trained at the facility.

Another person may have been awed by the talent at the Los Angeles Athletic Club, but not the brash and confident Keller. Victoria Draves and Sammy Lee were two of the resident divers. Draves won both the platform and springboard events in the 1948 Olympics and Lee won the Olympic gold medal in platform diving in 1948 and 1952. Patricia was strong, agile, spunky, and sure of herself, but terribly unpolished. Yet she placed second in the 1947 National Platform Championship and fourth in the 1948 Olympic tryouts, missing qualifying for the United States team by less than a point.

"That defeat was the greatest thing that ever happened to me because all of a sudden I knew I could win the Olympics. . . . I realized that at Los Angeles I was working with world-class athletes every day."

Patricia was soon at the top of the sport. In 1949, Pat married Glenn McCormick and competed under her married name. That year she won the National Platform championship. She repeated the victory in 1950 and added both the one-meter and three-meter springboard national titles. She won all five national titles in 1951, three outdoors and two indoors. McCormick became a consistent winner. She won 77 national titles and in her two Pan-American Games appearances she won the highboard in 1951, finishing second in the springboard, and won both the springboard and highboard in 1955.

Her most dramatic moment in sports came during the platform event in the 1956 Olympic games. She had already won three Olympic gold medals and grabbed the lead after three dives on her way to her fourth gold. Competition in those days began with four preliminary dives with the leaders progressing to a two-dive final round. McCormick completely missed the fourth dive and fell to second place behind teammate Paula Jean Meyers. Two Soviet divers were closing in at third and fourth place. A lesser competitor might have been overwhelmed by the pressure, but great ones come through in the clutch. The 28-year-old veteran hit her two final dives perfectly to win pulling away and lead a United States sweep of the event.

McCormick won the Sullivan Award in 1956 as the amateur athlete "who has done the most during the year to advance the cause of sportsmanship." She was only the second woman to win that award since its inception in 1930. Subsequently, five more women have been recipients. She also has been named the "Babe Zaharias Woman Athlete of the Year," the "Helms Hall of Fame North American Athlete of the Year," and the Associated Press' "Woman Athlete of the Year." She was the first woman diver to be elected to the International Swimming Hall of Fame.

In recent years Patricia McCormick has been seen regularly at diving competitions, particularly in Olympic years. Her daughter, Kelly, won a silver medal in springboard diving at the 1984 Los Angeles Olympics and earned a bronze medal in the same event in 1988. Kelly is the greatest of the modern American woman divers and, no other diver has a mother who has achieved the greatest feat in diving, the Olympic double-double.

Rosi Mittermeier

"Omi"
August 5, 1950–
Reit Im Winkl, West Germany

Rosi Mittermeier was a top-flight skier for over a decade who "never won the big one." Then at the end of her career when she was given little chance, Mittermeier won two of the three Olympic gold medals in alpine skiing and missed a yet-to-be accomplished triple by the narrowest of margins. She never gave up.

Alpine skiing consists of three events: the downhill, in which a skier descends a mountainside at nearly 60 miles per hour, the slalom, where competitors zigzag between gates as they work their way downhill, and the giant slalom, a combination of the other two events. Mittermeier, who was technically sound and therefore good at the slalom, did not have the natural speed to excel in the downhill.

Her first Olympic appearance came in 1968 at Grenoble, France as a 17-year-old novice. She finished twenty-fifth in the downhill, was disqualified in

Opposite: **Patricia McCormick, winner of an olympic "double-double" in diving (photo courtesy International Swimming Hall of Fame).**

the slalom and placed twentieth in the giant slalom. She was better in 1972 at Sapporo, Japan, with a sixth in the downhill, a seventeenth in the slalom and a twelfth in the giant slalom. She was good, but not great; these were hardly performances that people talk about years after a skier retires.

By 1976 she had matured and turned in a season that has yet to be matched. That year Rosi was 25, a seasoned veteran in a young person's sport, and known as "Omi," the German word for "Granny," to her fellow skiers. Her career at that point had been anything but spectacular. She began skiing on the World Cup circuit during the 1967–1968 season, the first year of competition. The World Cup schedule consists of approximately seven meets, mostly in Europe but also in North America. From 1967 through 1975 her World Cup record was:

Year	Downhill	Slalom	Giant Slalom
1967–71		(Did not place)	
1971–72		2 seconds	1 second
		1 third	
1972–73		1 first	
		2 seconds	
		1 third	
1973–74		2 firsts	
		1 third	1 third
1974–75		1 first	
	1 second		
	1 third	1 third	2 thirds

Mittermeier simply did not take skiing seriously, training hard enough to stay in shape but not to excel. In 1976, when she concentrated on the sport, she showed the world how good she really was.

She was merely another contender, and the oldest competitor at that, among the women alpine skiers who arrived at the Olympic Village at Innsbruck. But when she came down the mountain in 1:46.6 seconds to nose out prerace favorites Brigitte Totschnig of Austria and American Cindy Nelson in the downhill, she immediately became a media darling. "I had not the courage to look at the timing," she recalled. "I looked at the faces and I knew what I had done." In her ten-year career, Rosi had never won a downhill race. She succeeded this time because she skied a perfect race. The adrenalin was flowing.

A fine slalom racer for years, three days after her downhill victory she got the conditions a technical skier loves, an icy, fast course. Forty-two women competed in the Olympic slalom, but only 19 completed both runs without

Rosi Mittermeier winning her second gold medal at the 1976 winter Olympic games (photo courtesy *Ski Racing* Magazine).

missing a gate. Fellow West German Pamela Behr led after the first run, but Rosi was a slight .09 second behind. Behr fell to fifth on the final run while Mittermeier came back with the best time in the run to defeat Italian slalom specialist Claudia Giodani. The great Hanni Wenzel of Liechtenstein, who later won two golds and a silver in the 1980 Olympics, finished third. She said of the event, "With one gold in the pocket, things get easier."

She came close to a sweep but lost to another longshot, Kathy Kreiner, of Timmons, Ontario, by .12 second because she cut one gate a little too sharply. Mittermeier was so popular by then that even the parents of Kreiner said before the race, "Wouldn't it be a shame if someone prevented her from taking a triple." Little did they expect that their daughter would be the someone. But Rosi, ever the sportswoman, did not mind sharing the spotlight with a fellow winner. When asked about her disappointment, she replied, "It's not serious. I had one of my best giant slalom races ever." She and third-place finisher Daniele Debernard of France lifted Kreiner on their shoulders after the event.

Mittermeier was always one of the most popular skiers in competition. Once described as "having the smile of an angel and a devil's daring," she is a woman who has no illusions about herself. She was asked, "How could a very good skier like you suddenly attain greatness at the end of her career? Was it technical ability?" She responded, "I'd say no. . . .I now have concentration and I'm more relaxed. I love ski racing and since I am doing what I enjoy, I no longer worry about not doing well." Hank Tauber, director of the United States alpine team gave two reasons for her late success: "She has acquired the knack of finding the shortest way down the hill and. . .she is no stranger to failure and willing to take chances."

The year 1976 belonged to Mittermeier. In addition to her Olympic triumphs she was the World Cup overall winner while finishing first in World Cup slalom standings and second in the giant slalom. That season she won three slalom races and had two seconds and a third. She also won one giant slalom, had three seconds, and even placed third in a downhill.

Rosi hails from a tiny town, Reit Im Winkl, nestled in the Bavarian Alps in West Germany. She had a couple of near-fatal accidents as a youngster. When she was six months old a goat jumped into her baby carriage and she nearly suffocated. She accidentally ate a nearly-fatal dose of rat poison when she was two. Bad luck and injuries continued to plague her when she grew up. She was struck by a surfboard while on vacation in Hawaii in 1973 and missed most of a skiing season. In 1975, she collided with a tourist on the slopes and broke her arm. But her biggest obstacle was constantly fighting a case of the jitters at major events. She comes from a family of skiers. Both of her sisters, Heidi and Evi, competed for West Germany, and Evi eventually became one of the finest downhill racers in the world.

After the 1976 campaign she retired and demonstrated that she was also a fine businessperson. Her great smile, good looks, and wonderful personality made her a natural for product endorsements. She was not the finest skier who ever lived, but she had magic in her skis for one season. No one was ever a better sportsperson. People still cheer for Rosi.

Martina Navratilova

"It's good to compete"
October 18, 1956–
Prague, Czechoslovakia

Martina Navratilova was born in Prague, Czechoslovakia, in 1956 and grew up in Revnice, a Prague suburb. Her mother and father divorced when she was three. Her mother was from a wealthy Czech family that lost most of what it owned when Czechoslovakia was assimilated into the Soviet Union's sphere of influence. Her mother and second father were both tennis officials for the Czech government, and her grandmother was ranked number two in tennis in pre–World War II Czechoslovakia.

Martina's stepfather coached her as a child and guided her through the very competitive world of Czech youth tennis. At 14 she won her first national title in age-group competition, and by the time she was 16 she was the highest ranking female player in her homeland. Navratilova, at five feet, seven and one-half inches and 140 pounds, was the top tennis player in Czechoslovakia from 1972 until 1975.

Navratilova was always fascinated with geography, and delighted in the opportunity to visit foreign lands, particularly the U.S. She later said, "I didn't feel I belonged anywhere until I came to America for the first time when I was sixteen. . . I honestly believe I was born to be an American." On September 7, 1975, the 18-year-old Martina defected. She had the potential for greatness but lacked the temperament and desire to achieve it. She needed time to adjust to her newly-found freedom, away from the Czech tennis officials who had restricted her foreign play and frowned on her increasing Americanization. Unfortunately the teenager preferred fast foods to practice sessions and soon ate herself out of playing shape, gaining 20 pounds during her first months in the United States. She also let defeats upset her to the point that she frequently became distraught. Yet Navratilova was making an impact on the tennis world and was rated among the top five in the world from 1975 through 1977. She finally won her first major tournament, the 1978 Virginia Slims Championship in Oakland, and then went on to win the British Open title at Wimbledon with back-to-back victories in 1978 and 1979. She teamed with Chris Evert and Billy Jean King, respectively, to win the Wimbledon doubles title in 1976 and 1979 and added the 1979 Avon and Colgate Series championships to her growing list of victories. She was ranked first in the world in 1979.

Martina shows her aggressive backhand (photo courtesy Carol B. Newsom Associates/Virginia Slims).

Navratilova took charge of her emotions, eliminated a few flaws from her game, and totally dominated women's tennis during most of the 1980s. She made the British Open at Wimbledon her personal showcase, winning it nine times between 1978 and 1990, including six times in a row from 1982 through 1987. She added the French Open in 1982 and 1984 and won the United States Open four times and finished second four times between 1981 and 1987. Her 18 grand slam singles titles ranks fourth on the all-time list.

Navratilova also won the Australian Open in 1981 and 1983 and the Canadian National Championship back-to-back in 1983 and 1984. The Associated Press named her the "Female Athlete of the Year" in 1983. That year she played in 17 tournaments, won 16 of them, had 86 victories, and lost only to Kathleen Horvath in the round of 16 at the French Open.

The greatest money winner in women's professional tennis, at her peak, she was so good in tournament play that, at one point, she won 77 consecutive matches. Martina made headlines when she lost.

Navratilova was the greatest doubles player in the history of tennis. She and Pam Shriver won 20 grand slam titles, and for a two-year period, from the summer of 1983 until the summer of 1985, had a 109-match winning streak. Their overall record is 373–17, a .965 percentage, netting them over $2 million in purses. Martina won another ten grand slam doubles titles with other partners. As late as 1989 she won the United States Open doubles title with Hana Mandlikova.

King ruled the tennis world when Navratilova broke in, and was replaced by Evert as the ruling tennis queen. Martina assumed that title convincingly during the 1980s and held it until the emergence of Steffi Graf in 1988. Many tennis experts consider her to be the finest women's tennis player of the twentieth century. Her 145 singles titles support that position.

Much has been printed about Martina's personal life. She sums it up, "I have loved men and women in my life. . . . I'm even ambidextrous. I don't like labels. Just call me Martina." She loves to ski and feels that "sports are good for young women. It's good to compete, good to run, good to sweat, good to get dirty, good to feel tired and healthy and refreshed."

Diana Nyad
"Attempting the Impossible"
August 22, 1949–
New York, New York

Diana Nyad always seemed to attempt the impossible. She frequently achieved it.

The third of the great American distance swimmers, she followed in the wake of Gertrude Ederle and Florence Chadwick but accomplished some feats that the two who preceded her never even contemplated.

Diana Sneed was the daughter of a New York stockbroker, but her mother, Lucy, divorced William Sneed when Diana was three and married Aristotle Nyad, a land developer. Diana was raised in Ft. Lauderdale, Florida and spent much of her early life near the water. She began to take swimming seriously when she was 11 at about the time her mother's second marriage was dissolving. Her coach and middle school teacher, Jack Nelson, urged her to swim, and within two years she was excelling in the backstroke on the Florida age-group competition circuit.

Hopes of making the 1968 Olympic team as a backstroker were dashed when she contracted a virus infection of the heart in the spring of 1966. It took almost three years to recover fully, and she was never an effective short-distance swimmer again. Diana never got her speed back.

Then came a strange period in her life. She entered Emory College where she was an excellent student and pretty good swimmer, but just too wild for the school administration. Although naturally a serious person, Nyad sometimes cannot resist playing a practical joke or pulling off an unthinkable stunt. Parachuting from the fourth floor of one of Emory's dormitories was in the second category; she was expelled.

For a year she drifted through the United States and Europe, earning her way as a waitress and lifeguard. "I just wasn't ready for a life of work yet," she now admits. By 1970, she had reorganized herself and entered Lake Forest College in Illinois to begin some serious study and work on her swimming. She earned Phi Beta Kappa recognition and developed her innate talent. She loved the theater and took part in several presentations, studied English and French, played varsity tennis, and was a fine musician who played the piano and trumpet. During these college days she realized that she would enjoy the challenges that long-distance swimming provides.

Nyad inherited a most appropriate name from her stepfather. A naiad, as most crossword puzzle fans know, is a water nymph in classical mythology, a goddess who watches over springs, lakes, and fountains. In botany, it is a plant that thrives in water, an apt description.

Her long-distance swimming career as an amateur racer slowly evolved and she turned into a professional solo swimmer—the best woman long-distance racer in the world. In her first race in 1970, a ten-mile event on Lake Ontario, she finished tenth in a field of 160 men and women and was the first woman to wade ashore. Five years later she completed a solo swim across Lake Ontario, a 32-mile jaunt, in 20 hours. She was the first person to swim the route successfully.

Many of her marathon swims ranged up to 50 miles in the years between 1970 and 1975. The crocodile-infested Nile, the Suez Canal, the cold North and tropical Coral Seas were among the locales for these impressive conquests. Remarkably, she earned her bachelor's degree with honors from Lake Forest in 1973 and a master's degree in comparative literature from New York University while training for these swims.

Beginning in 1975, she undertook a series of marathon swims that were considered beyond human capability. In the fall of 1975 she attempted to swim around Manhattan Island. Although the distance is relatively short (for Diana Nyad), the 26-mile stretch of water is treacherous. The west side of Manhattan is bordered by the Hudson River, only a few miles before it empties into the Atlantic Ocean. That part of the river is strongly influenced by the tide that charges one way and then the other every six hours. The East River is on the east side of Manhattan. This body of water, which is actually a strait and not a river, connects the Hudson River with Long Island Sound. The confluence where the Sound meets the East River is known as Hell Gate because of the water turbulence. The rest of upper Manhattan is on the Harlem River, a relatively narrow creek crossed by a series of bridges that stir up the water that charges past them. The Harlem meets the Hudson at the northwest tip of Manhattan at a place known by its Dutch name, Spuyten Duyvil. Its story is that one old Dutchman who tried repeatedly to cross the river at this point swore he would do it "in spite of the devil."

Her first attempt on September 24, 1975, failed. Nyad was pulled from the water after six hours. She mistimed the tides and was actually losing ground for more than an hour. An off-shore hurricane had altered the time of the tides by several hours, creating an impossible situation. She shook off a virus apparently caused by the contaminated water and took her next plunge into the murky waters of the East River on October 6, 1975.

This time she would not be denied. Avoiding flotsam, becoming immune to the chilly 65-degree water, and singing "Row, Row, Row Your Boat," she

timed the tides perfectly and completed the loop in seven hours and 57 minutes, well ahead of the record established in 1927 by Byron Sommers. When she finished, she told her well-wishers, "I knew I'd make it. It's not easy to swim around this island, especially in October. This is my last time."

True to her word, Nyad never did swim around Manhattan Island again, but she continued to take on nearly-impossible challenges. Sometimes she made them sometimes she did not.

After a year in training came her next spectacular, the 103-miles from Cuba to Florida. Typically, she spent ten hours a day in the water to build her endurance and then spent additional time planning and promoting the swim. She loosened up each day by running ten sub-seven-minute miles. She had a special, motorized floating cage constructed to protect her from two potentially fatal enemies, sharks and Portuguese men-of-war. Confusion with the Cuban government in coordinating the attempt postponed the swim for several months. When she finally entered the water in August 1978, conditions were not ideal. Nyad was plucked from the water 42 hours later, still 60 miles from her destination. Jellyfish had sapped her strength and choppy seas and drifting had taken her far off course. Nyad's courage had been done in by a poorly-managed swim. The navigation was faulty, her floating cage turned out to be counter-productive, and the wind and weather forecasting were completely wrong.

The following year she was back at it again, this time for an attempt to swim from the Bahamas to Florida, a mere 89 miles. Her first attempt failed, but on August 19 and 20, 1979, she completed the swim in under 28 hours.

Nyad wrote a very literate autobiography, *Other Shores*, in 1978 and today works as a swimming analyst for ABC Sports. She is also a freelance writer whose byline is seen on a variety of topics in many periodicals. But her primary income today is derived from giving motivational lectures to corporate and school groups. These revolve around one theme: "If you put your guts into something, you'll do it."

Opposite: **Diana Nyad during her 1979 attempt to swim from Bimini to West Palm Beach (photo courtesy Wide World Photos).**

Annemarie Moser-Proell

"La Proell"
March 27, 1953–
Kleinarl, Austria

Since the World Cup alpine racing began in 1967, no woman has won the title more than twice—except one. Annemarie Proell was World Cup champion six times during the 1970s.

Annemarie came from a large family of eight children in the mountains of Austria. Her parents were farmers who worked hard to provide for the family. The entire family skied on the nearby slopes at every opportunity. When Annemarie was four, her father hand-whittled her first pair of skis. At times he must have regretted doing it when he saw his young daughter hurtling down the hills oblivious to the dangers. Annemarie never had formal skiing lessons when she was young; she developed her own style. It was not pretty but it got her to the bottom of the mountain faster than the competition.

Skiing became an obsession with Proell as she matured. She slipped away to the slopes instead of attending class on more than one occasion. At the age of fifteen she was slim and delicate and did not win many races. But by 1970 when she was 17, she was five feet, six inches tall and had matured to a powerful 150 pounds of fearless determination. For the next ten years she dominated alpine skiing to an extent that has not been approached by any other competitor.

Proell was the World Cup Overall Champion from 1971 through 1975. World Cup competition consists of the downhill, giant slalom and slalom. the events were held at six or seven different sites each winter during the 1970s. Proell's daredevil style and brute strength made her a tough competitor in the downhill event. During the five years between 1971 and 1975, she competed in 33 World Cup downhills against the finest skiers in the world, won 21 times and finished second on seven occasions. She won the giant slalom 11 times with four second-place finishes. She was not nearly as effective in the slalom, a finesse event, where she had two victories and four seconds during the five years. But as dominant as she was, her career had its disappointments.

Proell was favored to win the 1972 Olympic downhill at Sapporo, Japan. She had won five consecutive downhill races coming into the competition. But Marie Therese Nadig of Switzerland upset her in both the downhill and the giant slalom and Proell had to settle for two silver medals. After that disappointment, she attached a sign to the dashboard of her car that read, "Never Forget Sapporo." It took eight years to avenge that loss.

Her World Cup first, second, and third finishes from 1971 through 1975 are shown below:

Year	Number of races	Downhill			Giant Slalom			Slalom		
		1st	2nd	3rd	1st	2nd	3rd	1st	2nd	3rd
1971	6	2	2	0	3	1	1	2	0	0
1972	7	5	2	0	3	2	1	0	0	1
1973	7	7	0	0	0	0	0	0	0	0
1974	6	5	1	0	0	1	0	0	1	1
1975	7	2	2	1	5	0	0	0	3	0

After the 1975 season Proell retired; she was tired of the pressure, tired of the travel, and unhappy over the squabbling that frequently divided the Austrian national team. She married soccer player Herbert Moser and settled down to a quiet life. She spent the next year caring for her seriously-ill father, being a wife, and opening a bar-cafe that featured the finest pastries in Austria. She enjoyed the quiet life for a little more than a year and honestly did not miss competing in the 1976 Olympics.

Alpine skiing was not the same without her. Cindy Nelson, the best American woman downhill skier at that time and the bronze medal winner at the 1976 Games, once said, "I'd rather be second to Annemarie than win without her . . . it isn't the same. You knew you were up against the best." But skiing was in Moser-Proell's blood, and in the fall of 1976 she began training lightly. She finished behind Lise Marie Morerod in 1977 and Hanni Wenzel in 1978 for the overall World Cup championship, but the form was returning. The old Proell was back in 1979.

Moser-Proell dominated World Cup competition in the downhill during the 1978–79 season, winning six of the seven races contested. She also picked up a third and a second in the giant slalom and one second and three thirds in the slalom to nose out Wenzel for the overall championship. The winners of the overall World Cup crown during the 1970s are:

Year	Winner	Country
1970	Michele Jacot	France
1971	Annemarie Proell	Austria
1972	Annemarie Proell	Austria
1973	Annemarie Proell	Austria
1974	Annemarie Proell	Austria

Annemarie Moser-Proell, alpine skiing's greatest women's competitor, after another victory in 1971 (photo courtesy The Austrian Embassy).

1975	Annemarie Proell	Austria
1976	Rosi Mittermeier	West Germany
1977	Lise Marie Morerod	Switzerland
1978	Hanni Wenzel	Liechtenstein
1979	Annemarie Proell	Austria

By the time the 1980 Olympics were held, Moser-Proell's career was in decline. Then 27, an age generally considered too old for the rigors of alpine skiing, she entered the Olympics a decided underdog to Marie Therese Nadig, the woman who had upset her eight years before at Sapporo. She trained hard and kept her dashboard slogan in mind, "Never Forget Sapporo." She won the downhill at Lake Placid that year for her only Olympic gold medal, and she beat two of the best who have ever skied; Wenzel finished second and Nadig won the bronze.

Off the slopes Annemarie is a big, strong, determined German farm girl with relatively simple tastes. She loves pastry and, as a youngster, had a passion for racing cars and a general disregard for life and limb. Today she is a business woman. She hit the big time in alpine racing when she was 17 and was not yet emotionally mature enough to handle the hoopla. She developed a reputation of being curt with the press and somewhat of a braggart. She was once quoted as saying, "There is nobody who can beat me." All great athletes feel that way; she only expressed it openly.

After her marriage, she matured and adjusted to her celebrity status, yet she remains uncomplicated in her ways. The one-year break from the tension helped her.

The record book shows that Annemarie Moser-Proell is the top woman alpine skier of all time. In fact, no one is a close second.

Wilma Glodean Rudolph
"Skeeter"
June 23, 1940–
St. Bethlehem, Tennessee

Wilma Rudolph's sports career was relatively brief, yet there was never a finer, more graceful, nor more gracious athlete in the history of women's track and field. When she was a child, her doctors thought that Wilma would never walk, no less be a great champion.

Wilma Rudolph was born in St. Bethlehem, Tennessee, in 1940, the sixteenth of her father's 19 children, and grew up in rural Clarksville, Tennessee. Ed Rudolph was a retired railroad porter, Blanche, a domestic. Born prematurely at four and one-half pounds, each day of her first few months was a struggle to live. When she was four, Wilma suffered a severe attack of scarlet fever, complicated by double pneumonia, which left her unable to use her left leg. The medical verdict was that she would never walk, but her family did not

The power and grace of Wilma Rudolph winning the 400-meter relay at the 1960 Olympic games in Rome (photo courtesy Wide World Photos).

146   Wilma Glodean Rudolph

accept it. She was able to overcome her adversities because of the support her family gave her.

When Blanche Rudolph came home from work each day she massaged Wilma's legs for hours. She taught Wilma's brothers and sisters to do the massage so that Wilma received at least four daily massages for years. At eight she could walk a little with the aid of a specially-made shoe. When she was 11 she tossed away the shoe and had her first taste of sports competition, playing basketball with her brothers at their backyard hoop. Within a few months the boys on the street picked Wilma early when choosing sides to play three-on-three basketball.

The little kid who once had to sit and watch could play the game well. Rudolph averaged 32.1 points per game, a state record for high school girls basketball competition, as a sophomore at the all-black Burt High School in Clarksville. Her coach, Clinton Gray, was also the school's track coach, and he encouraged her to run. He also gave Wilma her nickname, "Skeeter," from the way she buzzed about a basketball court. Wilma enjoyed track and was delighted with the results. She was undefeated in running throughout high school. She made the United States Olympic track team in 1956 as a 16-year-old and won a bronze medal as a member of the 4-by-100-meter relay team.

Rudolph entered Tennessee State University in 1957 to work with famed track coach, Ed Temple. Coach Temple later modestly maintained that his only contribution to Wilma's success was to reduce the quantity of junk food she consumed, but he took raw talent and created a champion. Yet a series of injuries and illnesses kept her from reaching her full potential. Sickness kept her from competition in 1958; a severe pull in her left thigh finished her 1959 season; complications from a tonsillectomy threatened her participation in the 1960 Olympic games. But she was ready when the great athletes of the world convened in Rome that year.

At twenty Rudolph was one inch under six feet tall and had awesome power in her legs. When she ran, the power was barely noticeable, so effortless was her style. She glided so easily that one had to look twice to be sure her feet really touched the ground.

Wilma won the 100-meter Olympic dash by three yards after trying the world record in a preliminary heat. Her 11.0 seconds in the final would have been a world record, but the prevailing breeze was slightly above the allowable limit. She glided to an easy 200-meter victory, setting a new Olympic record of 23.2 seconds, just .3 second off her own world standard. She saved her best for the final event, the 4-by-100-meter relay.

The United States was represented in the relay by four women from the Tennessee State Tigerbelles, Barbara Jones, Lucinda Williams, Martha Hudson, and Wilma Rudolph, with Rudolph running the anchor leg. After her teammates handed her the baton with a slight lead, she broke the tape as the clock registered 44.4 seconds, a new world record. Rudolph, who 11 years before was still learning to walk, was recognized as the finest woman athlete in the world.

European sports fans, who had never before seen a woman athlete so graceful, skilled, and charming, were captivated. The French called her *La Perle Noire*, "the Black Pearl." She was "*La Gazzella Nera*" to the Italians. Americans just called her Wilma, and they knew that she was the greatest.

She competed successfully for a short period after her Olympic triumph. During the winter of 1961 she ran in the famous Milrose Games at Madison Square Garden in New York, the first time a woman had been invited to compete in the meet since the early 1930s. She tied the indoor record for 60 yards that night and established a new record two weeks later. That summer she lowered the standard for the 100-meter dash outdoors. Rudolph won the 1961 Sullivan Award as the nation's finest amateur athlete. But Wilma decided it was time to retire and do what she could to help others.

She married in 1961 and became a school teacher, coach, and mother to a family of four. Wilma is also the director of the Wilma Rudolph Foundation that provides opportunities for boys and girls to compete in sports in the Indianapolis area. During her many years working with young people it is evident that some of Rudolph's class has rubbed off on many of her charges.

Lydia Skoblikova
"Setting the standards of excellence"
March 8, 1939–
Zlatoust, Siberia, Soviet Union

North Americans became aware of speed skating when Eric Heiden swept the five events held for men during the 1980 Winter Olympics. As spectacular as this accomplishment was, it was not the first time that one competitor totally dominated the speed-skating events at the Olympics.

Lydia Skoblikova was the first superstar of speed skating. She was the standout of the 1960 winter games at Squaw Valley, the first year speed skating for women was an Olympic event. Skoblikova became the first woman to win an Olympic speed-skating gold medal when she won the 1500-meter event. She added the 3000-meter gold medal to her collection a few days later, and finished fourth in the 1000-meter race. Lydia did not compete in the 500 meters, the other speed skating event for women, yet she won the world title at that distance a few weeks later. But the 20-year-old Siberian was merely starting her career.

Out of international competition in 1961 and 1962, she began preparing to defend her Olympic laurels with an active 1963 campaign. She quickly demonstrated that she was the best speed skater in the world when she won all four women's titles at the world championships in Karuizawa, Japan. The stage was set for Innsbruck, Austria, in 1964.

Skoblikova won all four speed-skating races at the 1964 Olympics and established new Olympic records in three of the events. She was timed at 45.0 seconds at 500 meters, beating the old standard of 49.9, although she tripped and nearly fell on the second lap because the ice was beginning to melt. She broke her own record of 2:55.2 at 1500 meters by nearly 33 seconds and lowered the record for 1000 meters from 1:34.1 to 1:33.2. She hoped to skate the 3000 meters in a then unheard of sub-five minutes, but the new record was not to be. The ice at the arena was melting, and she had to skate through several puddles during each lap. Yet her time of 5:14.9 was four seconds faster than that of runner-up Valentina Stenina. Ever gracious and not one to make excuses, Skoblikova said afterwards, "The ice was perfect."

Lydia was the first person, man or woman, to win six gold medals in Olympic competition, and the first to win four at one Olympiad. She was rewarded for this accomplishment by being made a full-fledged member of the Communist Party. Premier Nikita Khrushchev personally notified Lydia of this honor.

Skoblikova went on to win the 1000-, 1500- and 3000-meter races at the 1964 world championships and, for the second consecutive year, was declared the women's speed-skating world champion.

Lydia was born in Zlatoust, a small town in the Ural Mountains, and has lived most of her life in Chelyabinsk, deep in Siberia. Finding ice time was never a problem, because winters are long and rinks plentiful in her part of the world. Her father was a metallurgical engineer, who was able to provide his daughter with the opportunity to skate and receive an education in the Soviet system. She began skating seriously when she was 12, and when she was 18, she married her trainer, Alexander Skoblikova, an instructor at Chelyabinsk Pedagogical Institute. Lydia also became a school teacher and specialized in anatomy.

Westerners were surprised with their first close-up look at the Siberian speed skater. She was a blue-eyed blonde who stood five feet, five inches tall and weighed a trim 126 pounds. When she smiled, which she did easily and often, she revealed a girlishly-warm but shy demeanor. She was almost as fond of music and literature as she was of skating. On the ice she was in a class by herself. She learned forward more obviously than do most skaters, with her upper body virtually parallel to the ice, holding that position whether she was gliding, in a full-out sprint, or maneuvering around the corners. Skoblikova had much of the showperson in her, and she endeared herself to the audience whenever she won an event. "I like to skate around the stadium after a victory. People applaud and that gives me pleasure. I enjoy being the best in the world," she said. She also enjoyed debunking the notion that Soviet women athletes were all well-muscled robots. "Skating makes us more feminine; cycling or skiing takes a lot of muscle, but skating does you no harm." When she told this to a reporter and gave him her pretty smile, he concurred.

At nearly 30 she was still skating competitively in the late 1960s and finished sixth at 3000 meters and eleventh at 1500 at the 1968 Olympic games. It was time to retire, continue teaching, and raise a family. She had established the standards of excellence at which speed skaters today still aim.

Irena Kirszenstein Szewinska

"First on the track?"
May 24, 1946–
Leningrad, USSR

Who was the greatest woman track athlete of all time? Many will answer Babe Didrikson or Fanny Blankers-Koen, perhaps Wilma Rudolph or Jackie Joyner-Kersee. A strong case may be made for Irena Kirszenstein Szewinska.

Irena Kirszenstein was born to Polish parents in the Soviet Union and competed for Poland internationally. She was as good and versatile an athlete as world-class track has ever seen. She appeared at five Olympic Games—Tokyo in 1964, Mexico in 1968, Munich in 1972, Montreal in 1976, and Moscow in 1980 and was a major factor in three of them.

She made her Olympic debut as an unknown 18-year-old at the 1964 Games and took home three medals. It took a record-setting effort by American Edith McGuire to nip her by one yard in the 200-meter final. Kirszenstein also finished second in the long jump when Mary Rand of Great Britain leaped 22 feet, 2 1/4 inches to establish a new world record. But Irena pocketed the gold in the 4-by-100-meter relay, the second leg in this stunning upset as Poland

Irena Szewinska, one of track and field's most versatile and enduring runners (photo courtesy Embassy of the Republic of Poland).

defeated a highly-favored American team. The clocking for the Polish team was an astonishing 43.6 seconds, a full .7 second faster than the existing world record. Three years later, the mark was disallowed when one of the team members failed to pass a sex chromosome test.

At the 1966 European Championships Kirszenstein starred. She won the 200-meter run and long jump, was second at 100 meters and was on the winning 400-meter relay team. It was the first of many times she would dominate a European track meet. She won a total of ten medals, five of them gold, at various European Championships.

Irena Kirszenstein married Janusz Szewinska in 1967. He became her husband and her coach.

In the 1968 Olympics she tied the world record at 11.1 for 100 meters in one of the trial heats but faltered slightly at the start of the final and finished third behind Wyomia Tyus and McGuire of the United States. It took an 11.0-second world record to beat her. Then it was her turn to set a world record at 200 meters in 22.58 seconds, well ahead of Australia's Raelene Boyle's second-place finish.

She progressed to the middle-distance events and, beginning in 1973, concentrated on the 400-meter run. Amazingly, she was better at this distance than at the sprints. She broke the 50-second barrier for 400 meters in 1973 in a new world record. It was only the second time she had competed in the event. Christina Brehmer of East Germany broke Irena's mark in early 1976, but Szewinska reclaimed it with a 49.75 later that year. The two record breakers met in Montreal during the 1976 Olympics to determine who was the best at the metric quarter mile.

Thirty-year-old Irena Szewinska, the mother of a seven-year-old boy, simply could not be outrun that July day in Montreal. She toyed with the field for 300 meters and then simply blew her competition away, winning by eight meters in the world-record time of 49.29. "I'm very happy," she said, "This was everything I was thinking about for years." She announced her retirement with these words, "These, I think, are the last Olympics for me."

She was not yet through. She qualified for the 1980 Polish Olympic team and competed in Moscow at the age of 34. She pulled up lame with a torn Achilles tendon while running a 400-meter heat and had to withdraw from the competition. This time her retirement was permanent.

Szewinska lived a quiet family life in Poland after leaving the competitive world. Like so many Eastern bloc athletes, she had a few more amenities than the average citizen.

Irena competed in five Olympiads over a 16-year period. She won seven medals in five different events and a complete set of medals—gold, silver, and bronze—at 200 meters. She set 11 world records: two at 100 meters, four at 200, three at 400, and two on 400-meter relay teams.

Wyomia Tyus

"The quiet sprinter"
August 29, 1945–
Griffin, Georgia

For too many years Wyomia Tyus was the Rodney Dangerfield of track and field; she simply got no respect. Only recently have people begun to realize that she accomplished as much as a sprinter as any other woman and as much as any man, with the exception of Carl Lewis and Jesse Owens.

A low-profile type of person who goes quietly about being the very best at what she does, she was not a born athlete and received little encouragement from her family. She first tried high jumping but could barely clear four feet. But she was a fighter who would never give up. She worked hard to develop her talent and became the best in the world.

Her father, a dairy worker, died when she was 15; her mother was a laundress in Griffin, Georgia. Wyomia, who had three older brothers, was the only athlete in the family and she gave little early indication that she would be a good one. Wyomia could only qualify for one varsity sport in high school, track and field.

Tyus was a good high school runner, but not a great one. But Ed Temple, who had guided Wilma Rudolph, saw her potential and invited her to a summer camp after she was graduated. She improved her techniques and earned a scholarship to Tennessee A and I, where Temple then coached. She quickly proved that Temple had a great eye for evaluating talent.

Much to everyone's surprise, Tyus qualified for the 1964 United States Olympic team as a 19-year-old sprinter. Her teammates at Tennessee, Edith McGuire and Marilyn White were considered better sprinters. Tyus's personal best time for 100 meters was 11.5, well off Wilma Rudolph's 11.0 that won the Olympics in 1960. She was primed for a top performance and won a preliminary 100-meter heat in 11.2, tying the world record. She cleanly beat Edith McGuire by two yards in the Olympic finals. Wyomia also won a silver medal at the 1964 games when she ran a leg on the U.S. 4-by-100-meter relay team. When Coach Temple began working with Wyomia he predicted, "by 1968 she will be unbeatable." She was four years ahead of schedule.

When the triumphant Tyus returned home to Georgia, her mother suggested that she retire from competition because she felt the running was "unladylike."

Although Wyomia had demonstrated that she was the fastest sprinter in the world in 1964, she continued to work hard to improve. The following summer, Wyomia broke her own world record for 100 meters with an 11.1 clocking and tied the world record for 100 yards at 10.3 seconds. During her career, she won five Amateur Athletic Union (AAU) titles, three at 100 meters and two at 200 meters. She also won the AAU indoor 60-yard title three times and was the winner of the 200-meter dash at the 1967 Pan Am Games. She was gearing up for the one feat that had eluded so many great sprinters, defending her 100-meter Olympic title.

The world has enjoyed watching many fine sprinters and Olympic champions. Rudolph, Owens, Valarie Borzov, Bob Hayes, Helen Stephens, Bobby Morrow, and Fanny Blankers-Koen all won the Olympic gold medal at 100 meters once; none successfully repeated. Archie Hahn, an American, won in 1904 and again two years later in 1906, but the 1906 games are generally considered unofficial.

The 1968 women's 100-meter championship was probably the most competitive in the history of the Olympic games. No fewer than five women shared the world record which stood at 11.1 seconds, and all five – Tyus, Irena Szewinska of Poland, Ludmila Samotyosova of the Soviet Union, and Barbara Ferrell and Margaret Bailes of the United States – were on hand at Mexico City. Ferrell, Bailes and Tyus set the tone by winning their opening round heats in 11.2 seconds, tying the Olympic record. Tyus ran a wind-aided 11.0 in the second round. Ferrell and Szewinska's 11.1 in that round tied the world record. The tortise was not going to win this final. The great Szewinska won one of the semifinal heats, Tyus the other. The Soviet, Samotoyosova, did not qualify for the finals.

Among the eight who lined up for the final gun were four world record holders, Chi Cheng, a future world-record holder from Taiwan, and Raelene Boyle, the Australian who finished no worse than fourth in the 100-meter dash for three consecutive Olympics and won two silver medals at 200 meters. It was the strongest field of women sprinters ever assembled. The pressure was on the defending champion, Tyus, who put herself further in the hole by false starting. One more false start and Wyomia would be a spectator. Tyus timed the starter's gun perfectly. Szewinska got off slowly. Exactly 11 seconds later Tyus was through the tape for a world and Olympic record and unprecedented back-to-back Olympic victories. Only Carl Lewis has since matched the feat.

Elated but ever modest, Tyus immediately announced her retirement: "I've

Opposite: **Wyomia Tyus winning the 1964 Olympic 100-meter dash in Tokyo. Teammate Edith McGuire (second from left) finished second (photo courtesy Wide World Photos).**

been quite fortunate and I think I'd like to retire a winner." First, however, there was one more big race to run. She anchored the American 4-by-100-meter relay team in winning a gold medal in the world-record time of 42.8 seconds.

Although no longer an active competitor, Wyomia Tyus is still a winner, devoting her life after track to education. Tyus feels that her most important accomplishment in life was earning her degree from Tennessee A and I. Currently a teacher in Los Angeles, she advises her pupils, "Sports is and will be only a part of your life, not all of it. It's good for women to be in the world of competitive sport so long as they don't get hung up on winning all the time."

Wyomia has two children and their education is her primary objective. "My goal is to get my kids into a good school and help them on their way to a good education. That's what it means to be part of a family."

Grete Andersen Waitz
"The maker of the marathon"
October 1, 1953–
Oslo, Norway

Grete Andersen was born in a section of Oslo known as Keyserlokka, the youngest of three children. Her mother worked in a local grocery store, her father at a vitamin factory. She was an outdoors person like most Norwegians and loved to swim, hike in the woods, and romp in the snow. Waitz recalls, "Those were good times, happy times." She joined a sports club when she was twelve and became interested in track competition. She was good, but never the best, because the races were at 60 or 100 meters, not her forte. She started winning when the distances got up to 300 meters and were run "cross country style." She was the national junior champion at 400 and 800 meters when she was 16.

A straight-A student in high school, she went to teachers college and became a grade school teacher while competing regularly in track and field. Grete's running career took off when she married Jack Waitz in 1975. Jack was a fine runner and had an accountant's logical business head. He convinced his wife that she was a better road than track runner and she proceeded to prove him correct. She won the world cross-country championship in 1978 the first of five times she earned the title. Her real distance, though, was the marathon.

Nina Kuscsik was the first woman to enter the New York marathon in 1970, and she did not finish. Beth Bonner of New Jersey in 1971 was the first to finish. Through 1977, the best finishing time for a woman was Miki Gorman's 2:39.11 in 1976. Waitz took over the New York event in 1978 and made it her personal workout. While Bill Rodgers and Alberto Salazar dominated the men's division (Bill won four times consecutively from 1976 through 1979 and Alberto followed with three straight victories from 1980 through 1982), Waitz was peerless in the women's division. She won all nine New York marathons in which she finished from 1979 through 1989.

The spectacle of women running more than 26 miles was a phenomenon that developed during her career. She qualified for both the 1972 and 1976 Norwegian Olympic team at 1500 meters but was not a finalist in either event. She was a fine middle-distance runner but could not compete with Lyudmila Bragina and Tatyana Kazankina of the Soviet Union and Grenheld Hoffmeister of East Germany at 1500 meters, the metric mile. They could not compete with Grete at long distances, but the international ruling bodies for athletics limited women's competition in those days to 1500 meters.

World records in the marathon are debatable. The distance is always the same — 26 miles, 385 yards — but the terrain varies. The traditional distance of approximately 26 miles is the length of the route from Marathon to Athens which a runner traveled to announce the Athenian victory over the Persians in the Battle of Marathon (490 B.C.). The actual distance of today's marathons was established during the 1908 London Olympic Games. Queen Alexandra (wife of Edward VII) wanted her children to see the start of the race at Windsor Castle, which happened to be 26 miles, 385 yards from the finish line at the Olympic stadium.

Waitz's first New York victory on October 22, 1978, a landmark day in women's sports, almost never occurred. She won the New York Marathon in world record time that day and demonstrated that women could run long distances and were interesting to watch. Her invitation to the meet was almost not sent because she insisted on receiving traveling expenses for her husband, and the New York track officials were only vaguely familiar with her reputation as a cross-country runner. Waitz had never run a marathon prior to New York and was a nobody among the entrants. The New York course was notoriously difficult, replete with potholes, hills, and too many bridges with irregular surfaces to establish a world record. The runner's miracle established the place of women in major marathons. Her world record, 2:32.30, was a full two minutes faster than the previous best. She lowered the world mark by four minutes and fifty-seven seconds in the following year's New York event. As recently as 1975, the accepted women's world record for the marathon was 2:40.16.

Grete Waitz, the great Norwegian distance runner who dominated the New York Marathon for more than a decade (photo courtesy Embassy of Norway).

Only New Zealand's Allison Roe and Priscilla Welsh of Great Britain interrupted Waitz's nine-victory streak over New York's pavements. The New York Marathon winners and their times from 1978 through 1988 were:

Year	Winner	Time
1978	Grete Waitz	2:32.30
1979	Grete Waitz	2:27.33

Year	Winner	Time
1980	Grete Waitz	2:25.41
1981	Allison Roe	2:25.29
1982	Grete Waitz	2:27.14
1983	Grete Waitz	2:27.00
1984	Grete Waitz	2:29.30
1985	Grete Waitz	2:28.34
1986	Grete Waitz	2:28.06
1987	Priscilla Welch	2:30.17
1988	Grete Waitz	2:20.07

The Olympic Games have been a jinx for Grete. She finished second to Joan Benoit at Los Angeles in the first Olympic Marathon for women in 1984. Severe leg cramps prevented her from finishing in 1988.

Her greatest race may have been in the 1988 New York Marathon. At age 35 she ran a 2:28.07 three months after arthroscopic surgery on her knee to defeat Benoit. It was only the second time that the two great marathoners had competed head-to-head. When asked if they had avoided each other, Grete responded, "She has her running plans; she has her injuries. I have my running plans, I have my injuries."

Waitz is characteristically serene, confident, and modest. She is the primary reason that women's distance running is taken seriously. Today the winner of the New York City Marathon wins an appropriate $26,385 and a Mercedes-Benz. A course record adds $10,000; a world record, $100,000. Grete Waitz was the key to making it all happen.

Kathryne Ann Whitworth

"A putter with a magic touch"
September 27, 1939–
Monahans, Texas

During the late 1960s a tall, lean Texan ruled the women's golf world. The five-foot-nine-inch, 140-pound champion became one of the two or three best woman golfers ever through hard work, incredible determination and a serene attitude. Looking at Kathy Whitworth, it is hard to believe her weighing 225 pounds and playing bass drum in the high school marching band.

A career total of 88 official victories on the Ladies Professional Golf Association (LPGA) tour puts Whitworth at the top of the list. Mickey Wright is second with 82, and only Patty Berg, Betsy Rawls, and Louise Suggs have more than 50 victories. It is unlikely that anyone will ever surpass her total.

She played well for two reasons: She never lost her nerve, and her putter had a magic touch. She simply never three-putted. Sandra Haynie, one of her top rivals, said of Whitworth, "When she has to putt, she gets it every time." Fellow professional, Carol Mann, adds, "She is the best under pressure of anybody who ever played on the tour."

The magic did not come easily for Kathy. She was born in Monahans, Texas, but grew up in Jal, New Mexico, where her father owned a hardware store. She took up golf at 15 primarily to take off weight. Although she was a fine natural athlete, golf seemed foreign to her and she developed an interest in it mostly because she found it difficult.

"Sports has always come naturally to me," she once said, "but golf created quite a challenge." She began playing in amateur tournaments in 1955 and had moderate success locally. The 18-year-old went on the professional tour in 1958 and fell on her face; she could not win. Self-conscious about her hefty 170 pounds, the lack of self-confidence led to poor play. Whitworth quit the game for a year and one-half, got down to a slim 140 pounds, and went back on the road. Her earnings were exactly $33 after six months on the tour. She broke into the winner's circle in 1962 by winning the Kelly Girl Open and the Phoenix Thunderbird Open. In 1963, she got her game together and won eight tournaments, but in 1964, she slumped badly, winning only once. From 1965 until well into the 1970s Kathy dominated the tour. Her tournament record for those years was:

Year	Victories	Year	Victories
1965	8	1970	6
1966	9	1971	5
1967	8	1972	5
1968	10	1973	7
1969	3		

She added 14 more titles between 1974 and 1984.

Kathy Whitworth won the Vare Trophy for the lowest annual average score on the LPGA tour seven times. She was the leading money winner eight times, including every year from 1965 through 1973 except 1969 when Mann edged her. Her greatest frustration was that she never won a United States Open, but she did win the LPGA title three times.

She was selected "LPGA Player of the Year" in every year from 1966

Kathy Whitworth, the most consistent winner on the LPGA Tour (photo courtesy Ladies Professional Golf Association).

through 1973, except 1970. The Associated Press picked her as "Woman Athlete of the Year" in 1965 and 1967.

Purses for LPGA tournaments were small when Whitworth was at her peak. From 1982 through 1988 the total LPGA purse was more than double the combined prizes from 1950 through 1981. In 1984, helped by the increased purses, she became the first woman to win more than $1 million on the tour. Kathy was one of the primary forces behind the LPGA's quest for greater purses and was president of the Association in 1967, 1968 and 1970.

In her later years on the tour, Whitworth set one milestone after another. In 1975 she was inducted into the LPGA Hall of Fame. As noted, she became the first $1 million career earner in 1981. In 1982 she tied Wright for the most tour victories at 82 and later that year became the all-time leader with the Lady Michelob tournament. In 1984 she broke Sam Snead's record for most all-time tournament victories when she defeated Rosie Jones in a play-off to cop the Rochester International title.

Kathy has always been one of the most popular professionals away from the links. She is easy-going and personable, yet she never became a well-known celebrity because she displayed little charisma on the course. She played methodically, hit the ball long and putted with the best, yet she never entertained the galleries. "I'm not colorful," she once suggested, although she was the model of consistency, coolness, and concentration on the course. All she could do was win.

Katarina Witt

"Carmen"
December 1965–
Karl-Marx-Stadt (Chemnitz), East Germany

The long-held stereotype of East German woman athletes was not flattering: "big shoulders...steroid users...amazons...robots...." They are not really women.

There is little questioning that the East German training methods produced many of the most powerful modern women athletes. But the system's premier product is the beautiful, talented, and captivating Katarina Witt.

Only Sonja Henie has dominated women's figure skating for a longer period than Witt. Her ability to stay at the top for nearly a decade during the 1980s is truly remarkable.

At 14 years old she had her first taste of big-time international competition in 1980. She could do no better than tenth in the world competition then, but the next year she placed fifth, and in 1982, she finished second in the world meet and won the European title. From 1984 through 1988, Katarina was clearly on top in the figure-skating world.

The 1984 Olympics was supposed to belong to two Americans, Rosalynn Sumners and Elaine Zayak. Sumners was the United States champion from

1982 through 1984. Zayak won the world title in 1982 but was nosed out by Sumners in 1983.

Olympic figure-skating competition is now composed of three segments; compulsory figures, in which the skaters trace randomly selected designs on the ice; a short program which must contain specific maneuvers, and a free-skating program. The free skating is held last and constitutes 50 percent of the score.

Zayak did poorly in the compulsory figures, normally Witt's weakest event. This time she was third to Sumner's first after that phase of the competition and inched ahead of her American rival in the short program. Katarina skated a dazzling free-skating program that was just good enough to edge Rosalynn.

From her success in the 1984 Olympics until her retirement as an amateur after the 1988 season, Witt lost only one competition. That took place in Geneva, Switzerland, at the 1986 World Figure-Skating Championships when Debi Thomas of the United States scored an upset. The East German was unsurpassed through the competition at the European and world championships in both 1984 and 1985. In 1987 she put on her finest performance at the world competition in Cincinnati, Ohio, to win back the title. She placed first on the scorecards of seven of the nine officials. The stage was set for the two skating stars, Thomas and Witt, to battle it out for the 1988 Olympic gold medal.

Thomas placed second in the compulsory figures at the Olympics and Katarina was a close third. Witt moved into first place after the short program. In the much ballyhooed "Battle of the 'Carmens'" (both competitors skated to the music of "Carmen"), Witt skated an exceptionally beautiful but conservative program that left the door open for Thomas to win. But then Thomas missed several of her jumps and finished third. Commentator Phil Hersh summed up the competition this way: "Thomas skated brilliantly to Carmen, Witt is Carmen." Witt retired after defeating Thomas again at the world championships at Budapest that March.

Witt's style is unusual and stunningly surprising for someone trained in the East German system. A notoriously poor performer at practice sessions, she turns on the energy when she is in front of an audience. She flirts with the audience and judges as she skates and interprets the music in a seductive, sexy style. She once said, "When you are on the ice and the audience is with you and you can hear the music and express the music, it is so much more than a sport. . . I want to be remembered as starting a new era in figure skating where one tries to express the music, tell the whole story."

Katarina is an interesting blend of East and West. She was a firm believer in the East German training system and is convinced that she would not have had the same opportunities to excel in the West. She was one member of the East German Communist party who liked to wear Western jeans, listen to rock

Katarina Witt, ice skating superstar (photo courtesy Wide World Photos).

music, and drive European sports cars. She studied acting and hopes to have a successful screen career. She began skating professionally in ice extravaganzas in 1989 with her government's approval. When the Berlin Wall collapsed she was free to become a full-fledged professional and seized the opportunity.

Witt and Olympic champion Brian Boitano created a new form of entertainment in late 1988 with their exploits on ice. First came a Christmas television special, "Carmen on Ice," that received rave reviews. They then put together a sophisticated road show, "Brian Boitano and Katarina Witt Skating," which had a successful 30-city, 30-performance tour. Witt will be a star for years, and ice-skating audiences will continue to be thrilled by her performances.

Mary Kathryn Wright

"Mickey"
February 14, 1935–
San Diego, California

Those looking for the greatest woman golfer of all time might consider Mickey Wright's career.

Wright won 82 tournaments in 25 years, 75 of them during 12 seasons from 1957 through 1968. From 1956 through 1969 she won at least one title each year. She won her last tournament in 1973 when she was 38 and her record of 82 victories was topped in 1983 when Kathy Whitworth won her eighty-third title.

Unlike Whitworth, Wright made a habit of winning the big ones. She won the United States Open in 1958, 1959, 1961, and 1964 and was runner-up in 1968. She took the Ladies Professional Golf Association (LPGA) title in 1958, 1960, 1961, and 1963 and was runner-up in 1964 and 1966. She also won the Vare Trophy for the lowest annual average score on the professional tour five, consecutive years from 1960 through 1964 and shot a sensational 62 in 1962 in a professional tournament in Midland, Texas.

Although she was the leading money winner in women's golf from 1961 through 1964, Wright hardly became rich because the purses were so low. Her winnings during her peak years were:

Year	Earnings
1961	$22,000
1962	21,000
1963	31,000
1964	29,000

Today, runners-up receive more money for one tournament than Mickey Wright earned in a year. She took home $31,000 in 1963, and had won 13 tournaments.

Women golfers have made significant progress since the 1960s. the first LPGA skins game played in May of 1990 earned Jan Stephenson $200,000 for sinking one putt for a par on the seventeenth hole. Fellow competitors Nancy Lopez, Joanne Carner, and Betsy King took home a total of $250,000 among them.

Most observers consider 1961 to be Wright's most successful year. She completed a grand slam of the major women's tournaments that year by capturing the LPGA, United States Open and Titleholders title. The Titleholders was the LPGA equivalent of the men's Masters tournament.

Whether she is the best woman golfer of all time, she certainly was the longest hitter. Wright's drive averaged 225 yards off the tee and she frequently cranked it up to 270. Golf legend Gene Sarazan tells of seeing her reach over 300 yards. "I never thought I'd see a woman hit the ball 300 yards, but I saw Mickey do it in Portugal. She hit several drives that would have been a credit to the men pros." On one occasion, with a strong wind at her back, Wright overdrove the green on a 385-yard hole.

Hailing from San Diego, California, a cradle of sports champions, her father, an attorney, started her playing golf when she was nine. He gave Mickey her nickname because he had wanted a boy he planned to name Michael. When she was 11, Mickey shot a 145 but then improved dramatically. She broke 100 at 12, shot 80 at 13, and scored a 70 in a tournament when she was 15. Mickey had an image problem as a teenager because she was a big girl and had to live with the nickname, "Moose." She took out her frustrations on the golf ball. She blossomed into a tall and powerful five-foot-nine-inch, 150-pounder with blue eyes and blond hair.

Wright entered Stanford University in 1952 to study psychology and play golf but left in 1954 to become a professional golfer. She was good from the start. When Babe Didrikson saw the 19-year-old swing she gave high praise for her: "I didn't think anybody but the Babe could hit 'em like that." Within two years Babe was dead and Mickey was the best woman golfer in the country. She dominated the game through the mid–1960s but was forced into semiretirement by a persistent nerve condition in her feet that eventually

Mickey Wright, one of the early LPGA stars and the dominant player of the 1960s (photo courtesy Ladies Professional Golf Association).

required two operations. She played occasionally in the 1970s and appeared at several "Legends of Golf" tournaments in the 1980s in which she completed her rounds using a golf cart.

The Associated Press's "Woman Athlete of the Year" in 1963 and 1964, in 1964 she was elected to the LPGA Hall of Fame. The Women's Sports Foundation elected her to the International Women's Hall of Fame in 1981. Wright, who lives in Port St. Lucie, Florida, said of her retirement from the game: "I like the way my life is now but quitting a sport is like quitting cigarettes. It ain't easy. I had some nice times and some wonderful memories." So did the galleries who watched her.

Sheila Grace Young

"Two Sport World Champion"
October 14, 1950–
Birmingham, Michigan

A world champion in two sports at the same time—Sheila Young earned that rare honor by winning a world championship in both speed skating and cycling in 1973.

Even the great, versatile athletes of the past never achieved this feat. Jim Thorpe was a double Olympic gold-medal winner, the finest football player of his era, and a seven-year major league baseball player. Babe Didrikson was the finest woman basketball player of her day, the winner of two Olympic gold medals, and the finest woman golfer of her era. Yet neither of these two sports giants held world titles in two different sports simultaneously. Even when Eric Heiden, the greatest speed skater ever, competed in cycling, he was no better than a good competitor.

Both of Young's parents were cyclists and speed skaters, sports that require similar training methods. She started skating at two, and, although her whole family were avid participants, she was not pushed into competition and did not compete seriously until she was 13.

Sheila suffered a great loss when she was 12: Her mother died of cancer and her dad was left to raise the family of four children. He moved to Detroit to find better employment. Sheila never felt comfortable with the new school and environment and began to channel her energies into skating. She received plenty of support, sincer her brothers, sister, and father spent as much time as they could at the local ice rinks. Sheila's dad was quoted as saying, "Going skating went with raising the kids. I couldn't afford a babysitter, so everybody had to come along."

Speed-skating competition is relatively new. The first Olympic events for women were held in 1960 at Squaw Valley, the year the United States Outdoor Championships for women were first conducted. Men have been speed skating in the Olympics since 1924.

Every Olympic speed-skating gold medal through 1968 had been won by women from the Soviet Union, East Germany, the Netherlands, or Finland, but the United States was developing some stars. Jeanne Ashworth from Massachusetts won a bronze medal at 500 meters in 1960. Soviet skater Ludmila Titova won the 500-meter race in 46.1 seconds in 1968, and three American girls, Jennifer Fish, Dianne Holum, and Mary Meyers, all tied for second at 46.3

seconds. Dianne also won a bronze medal at 1000 meters and enthusiasm for the sport began to develop.

United States skaters have always been hampered by a lack of facilities to develop world-class speed skaters. The only appropriate arena in Sheila Young's time was in Northbrook, Illinois, a Chicago suburb, where long-time speed-skating enthusiast, Ed Rudolph, the park commissioner, oversaw the construction of a marvelous facility. By 1972, a Northbrook native, 16 year-old Anne Henning, joined with Dianne Holum to form a powerful American duo. Henning, the sprinter, won the 500 meters in Olympic-record time and placed third at 1000 meters. Holum, the durable one, won the gold at 1500 meters and was second at 3000 meters.

Young, still relatively inexperienced at international competition although she was 21, finished fourth at 500 meters. Coming so close to a medal was the incentive she needed to push herself to be a world champion. In 1973 Young had one of the finest years any athlete has ever achieved. She was coached by Peter Schotting, who replaced her father, and the more professional coaching began to pay off. Since speed skating and cycling were amateur sports, Sheila's father continued to pay the bills. "This sport keeps me broke," he once said, "but this is what kept my family together. . .and I love it."

Sheila opened the year by winning the 500-, 1000-, and 3000-meter races at the United States speed-skating championships. The 3000 meter event was a remarkable victory for a person considered a sprinter. Her strongest feature was her explosive start. Later that month, she set the world record for 500 meters at 41.8 seconds, competing at Davos, Switzerland. In February she completed her skating season by becoming the women's world champion at 500 meters. Now it was time to put away the skates and hop on the bicycle. Other championships were waiting to be won.

Sheila Young was just another cyclist when she entered the 1973 world cycling championships in San Sabastian, Spain. Cycling was a European sport. No American, man nor woman, had won a world cycling championship since the early 1920s. Moreover, Galina Ermolasva of the Soviet Union was on the scene and she had already won the world sprint-cycling championship six times. But Galina had not yet met a performer with Young's heart.

In the preliminary heats, Sheila cracked up her bicycle twice. Her arms and legs were cut and the trackside doctor had to use a clamp to stem the bleeding from Sheila's head. Yet she finished first in the finals to win the world sprint championship and achieve her unique double. As one writer put it, "Sheila's victory was a tribute to her courage as well as her skill."

She then began preparing for her next goal, winning an Olympic gold medal in speed skating. She could not win one in cycling because the sport was

Sheila Young, the only athlete to win a world championship in two different sports in the same year (photo courtesy Clair Young).

considered too dangerous for women. Women's cycling was added to the Olympic agenda in 1984.

Young won the women's speed-skating world sprint title in 1975 and lowered the world 500-meter record to 40.91 seconds in early 1976. She was ready for the Winter Olympics at Innsbruck, Austria, in February 1976.

Young shared the spotlight with Dorothy Hamill as the stars of the 1976 games. She won a complete set of medals—gold at 500 meters where she set an Olympic record, silver at 1500 meters, and bronze at 1000 meters. She was the first American athlete, man or woman, to win three medals at a single Winter Olympiad.

Later that year she successfully defended her world sprint championship, her third title in four years. She then lowered the world mark for 500 meters to 40.68 seconds. That summer she won both the United States and world sprint-cycling championships.

Sheila's double world championship is a challenge for other athletes to match. So far no one has done it.

Appendix: The Greatest Woman Athlete of All Time

Babe Didrikson (photo courtesy Lamar University).

Mildred Ella "Babe" Didrikson Zaharias

Basketball All-American — 3 times
Olympic Gold Medalist — 80-meter hurdles
Olympic Gold Medalist — javelin throw
Olympic Silver Medalist — high jump
U.S. Women's National Team track champion — 1932
Women's British Amateur golf champion
U.S. Women's Open golf champion — 3 times
Chosen "Greatest Female Athlete of the First Half of the 20th Century" by Associated Press

Index

Aaron, Henry 77
AAU 11, 56, 57, 66, 155
Acker, Carl 122
Albright, Tenley 62–65, 107, 110–111
Altwegg, Jeanette 62
Amateur Softball Association 114
American Academy of Achievement 65
ancient world 1–2
Anheuser-Busch Brewing Company 106
Annie Get Your Gun 50
Aquacade 39, 43, 71
Arabian American Oil Company 72
archery 2, 5, 33
Armstrong Stadium 103
Astaire, Fred 18, 119
Astor, Lady 25
Atlantic City 121
Austin, Tracy 92
Australian Day Council 15
Australian Swimming Union 15
Australian tennis 81–85, 92, 101–103
aviation 34–37

Bahamas 141
basketball 11
Bath 32
Bausch and Lomb Championship 103
Behr, Pamela 133
Benoit, Joan 65–68, 159
Berg, Patty 7, 36, 160
Berlin, Irving 50
bicycle riding 4
Bingley, Branch 32, 3
Blankers-Koen 5, 7, 69–71, 150, 155
Bloomer, Amelia 4
Bonner, Beth 157

Boston Deaconness Hospital 65
Boston Marathon 66–68
Bowdoin College 65, 66
Bowie Race track 120
bowling 2–3
Boyle, Raelene 152, 155
Bragina, Lyudmila 157
Brehmer, Beth 157
Brighton Beach 38
Briscoe, Valarie 105
British Commonwealth Games 13, 15
Brooklyn College 114
Browne, Mary Kimball 28
Brundage, Avery 42–43
Brunet, Pierre 110
Budd, Zola 87–88
Budge, Don 101, 103
Buffalo Bill 48–49
Burka, Petra 96
Burt High School 147
Busch, Gundi 64
Butler, Frank 48
Button, Dick 18, 96, 110
Byrd, Admiral Richard 36

Campbell, Dorothy 28
Cap Gris-Nez 37, 39, 72
Capriati, Jennifer 103
Carlton Club 24
Catalina Island 72
Catherwood, Ethyl 5
Chadwick, Florence 71–74, 138
Chambers, Dorothea Lambert 45
chariot races 1
Cheng Chi 155
Chicago Marathon 68

Churchill Downs 119
Clifton, Sweetwater 99
Collett, Glenna 28–31, 60
Columbia University 35
Comaneci, Nadia 74–77
Connecticut Falcons 104
Connolly, Maureen 78–81, 94, 100
Connors, Jimmy 94
Coolidge, Calvin 39
Cooper, Chuck 99
Cordero, Angel 121
Cosmopolitan Tennis Club 97
Cotton, Henry 60
Court, Margaret Smith 7, 81–85, 91, 100, 101, 115, 117
Crapp, Lorraine 13
Cresta bobsled run 33
croquet 3, 33
Cuba 141
Cummings, Edith 28
Curtiss Cup 31
Cuthbert, Beth 7

Davis, Willie 32
Davydova, Yeleva 77
Decker, Mary 8, 85–88
de Coubetin, Baron 5
de la Roche, Baroness 34
de Leeuw, Dianne 108, 109
Dempsey, Jack 78
Derek, Bo 74
Didrikson, Babe 5, 6, 7, 10–12, 19, 32, 57, 115, 150, 173
diving 128–131
Dod, Lottie 6, 32–33
Dorffeldt, Ilse 56
Dorsey, Francis 64
Dover 72
Draves, Victoria 128, 129

Earhart, Amelia 34–37
East River 139
East St. Louis 19
Eaton, Dr. Hubert 99
Ederle, Gertrude 11, 37–40, 71, 72, 138

Eisenhower, Dwight 12, 74
Eisenhower, Mamie 81
Emory College 138
Employers Casualty Insurance Company 11
Ender, Kornelia 88–91
Engel-Kramer, Ingrid 28
English Channel 37–40, 72
equestrian team 53
Errath, Christina 108, 109
Evert, Chris 83, 91–94, 100, 101, 103, 135

Fassi, Carlo 96, 107, 109
fencing 3
Ferrell, Barbara 155
field hockey 33, 65, 66
Fishwick, Dianne 30
Fitzwilliam Club 3
Fleming, Peggy 5, 16, 94–97, 107, 109, 110
Fletcher, Ken 84
Florida A and M 99
Foley, Brian 109
Forest Hills 23, 24, 99, 100, 116
Fraser, Dawn 7, 13–15
Fraser, Gretchen 122
Fratianne, Linda 109
Fry, Shirley 78, 101

Gallico, Paul 24, 38
Gardiner, Winthrop 18
Garmisch-Partenkirchen 18
Garrison, Zina 103
Gehrig, Lou 38
Gibson, Althea 97–100
Giodani, Claudia 133
golf 2, 4, 5, 6, 28–31, 58–60, 125–128, 159–162, 165–168
Goodwill Games 20
Goring, Herman 43
Gorman, Miki 157
Gould, Shane 13, 88
Graf, Steffi 100–103, 115
Gray, Clinton 147
gymnastics 74–77

Hamill, Dorothy 107–109
Harlem 98–99
Harlem Globetrotters 99–100
Harper's Bazaar 118
Hart, Doris 78, 101
Harvard Medical School 65
Hayes, Helen 42
Haynie Sandra 160
Heathcote-Amory, Lady *see* Wethered, Joyce
Heiden, Eric 148
Heiss, Carol 64–65, 91, 107, 110–112
Henie, Sonja 3, 5, 6, 15–19, 107
Hepburn, Audrey 97
heptathlon 19–22
Heraean Games 1
Hill, Dorothy Poynton 128
Hitler, Adolf 56, 57
Hoffmeister, Grenheld 157
Holiday Park Tennis Club 91
Holm, Eleanor 40–43, 71
Holmes, Dorothy 107
Hoover, Herbert 36
horses 3, 52, 53, 118–122
Horvath, Kathleen 137
House of David 12
Howell, Linda Scott 2
Howland Island 37
Hudson River 139

ice skating 3, 5, 15–18, 62–65, 94–97, 107–109, 110–112, 148–150, 162–165, 168–172
Illinois Women's Athletic Club 11
International Federation Cup 92
International Swimming Hall of Fame 43, 90, 131
International Women's Hall of Fame 33, 34, 43, 82, 94, 115
Irish Sea 74

Jacobs, Helen 24, 45, 100
Jarrett, Art 42
Jenkins, David 112
Jesse Owens Award 22, 82

Jesse Owens National Youth Games 104
Joan of Arc 2
Johansson, Greta 128
Jones, Barbara 147
Jones, Bobby 31, 58
Johnson, Fred 97
Johnson, Dr. Robert 99
Joyce, Joan 8, 112–115
Joyner, Al 20, 106
Joyner, Florence 5, 8, 19, 91, 104–106
Joyner-Kersee, Jackie 19–22, 106, 115, 130

Karolyi, Bela 77
Kellerman, Annette 38
Kelley, Mile-a-Minute 4
Kersee, Bob 20, 106
Khrushchev, Nikita 149
Kim, Nellie 76
King, Billy Jean 7, 47, 81, 84, 91, 100, 101, 115, 116, 135
Kingsdorn 39
Knight, Ray 127
Korbut, Olga 76
Kreiner, Kathy 133, 136
Kristiansen, Ingrid 68
Krone, Julie 118–121
Kuscsik, Nina
Kusner, Kathy 119

La Jolla 71–72
Lake Forest College 138
Lake Michigan College 119
Lake Ontario 74, 139
Lake Placid 62
Laurel Park 121
Laver, Rod 101
Lawrence, Andrea Mead 122–124
Lee, Gypsy Rose 74
Lee, Sammy 129
Leitch, Cecil 28
Lenglen, Suzanne 6, 23, 24, 43–47, 100, 103, 115
Lewis, Carl 153, 155
Lie, Arnie 18

Lindbergh, Charles 34, 36
Lloyd, John 94
Long Island Sound 139
Lopez, Nancy 125–128
Los Angeles Athletic Club 129
Lott, George 103
Louganis, Greg 128
Loughran, Beatrix 15
LPGA 7, 12, 31, 100, 115, 127, 160,
   161, 162
Lynn, Janet 107

McArthur, Charles 42
McCormick, Kelly 131
McCormick, Patricia 128–131
McGuire, Edith 150, 152, 153
Madison Square Garden 18, 46, 110,
   148
Magnussen, Karen 107
Maine 65, 68
Mallory, Molla 46, 52
Manhattan Island 2, 139, 141
Mann, Carol 160
marathon running 65–68, 71–74,
   156–159
Marble, Alice 100, 115
Mary, Queen of Scots 2
Mazur, Bill 103
Meadowlands 119, 121
Melton, Tim 127
Meyers, Paula Jean 129
Middle Ages 2
Mittermeier, Rosi 131–134
Moffitt, Billy Jean see King, Billy Jean
Moffitt, Randy 115
Moody, Helen Wills see Wills, Helen
Moser-Proell, Annemarie 142–145
Moses, Phoebe see Oakley, Annie
Moore, Burt 54
Mota, Rosa 68
Motley, Marion 99
Muscle Beach 129

Nadig, Marie Therese 142, 144, 145
National Geographic Society 36

National Horse Show 53
National Softball Hall of Fame 115
Navratilova, Martina 100, 101, 102, 103,
   115, 118, 135–137
NCAA 20, 104–105
Nelson, Cindy 132, 143
New Orleans 3
New York University 112, 139
New York World's Fair 39, 43, 71
Newport, Rhode Island 3, 52, 53, 87
Nicklaus, Jack 60
Nile River 139
Noonan, Fred 37
Nunn, Glynis 20
Nyad, Diana 138–141

Oakley, Annie 3, 47–50
Olympics 1, 2, 3, 5, 11, 13–19, 22, 24,
   38, 40–43, 54–58, 62–65, 66–68,
   69–71, 76–77, 89–91, 94–97, 101,
   103, 104–106, 128–131
Orange Lionettes 114
Oustad, Niles 18
Outerbridge, Mary 3
Owens, Jesse 57, 153

Pan Am Games 20, 87, 129, 155
pentathlon 19–22
Perry, Fred 84
Persian Gulf 72
polo 53
Prince of Wales 54
Purdue University 36
Putnam, George 36
Pyle, C. C. 46

Quakers 47
Queen Elizabeth 81
Queen Victoria 2, 32, 50

Radcliffe College 65
Radke, Lina 5, 66
Rand, Mary 150

Index

Rawls, Betsy 160
Raybestos Brakettes 114
Reichart, Ossi 124
Renshaw, William 33
Richards, Vinnie 80
Riggs, Bobby 7, 116–118
Robin Hood 2
Robinson, Elizabeth 54
Robinson, Jackie 99
Robinson, Sugar Ray 97, 104
Roe, Allison 68, 158, 159
Roman Era 1
Roosevelt, Eleanor 36
Rudolph, Wilma 5, 145–148, 150, 153
Ryan, Elizabeth 47
Ryan, Nolan 112

Sabatini, Gabriela 101, 103
St. Andrew's 2, 58
St. Moritz 18, 33, 122
San Francisco Western Women's Club 11
Scotland 2
Scott, Barbara Anne 107
Sears, Eleonora 50–54
Seles, Monika 103
Sells Brothers Circus 48
Seyfert, Gabriele 101, 103
sharpshooting 47–50
Shaw, George Bernard 25
Shriver, Pam 137
Shula, Trixi 107
Sitting Bull 48, 50
Skating Club of Boston 62
skiing 122–125, 131–134, 142–145
Skoblikova, Lydia 148–150
Smith, Margaret see Court, Margaret
  Smith
Smith, Robyn 119
softball 112–115
Sparta 1
Spitz, Mark 38
squash 53
Staten Island 3, 8
Stenina, Valentina 149
Stephens, Helen 54–58, 65, 155
Stetson, Helen 28, 30
Stevenson, Sandra 18

Stirling, Alexa 28
Stouter, Sharon 13
Strickland, Shirley 70
Stultz, Wilmer 36
Suggs, Louise 160
Sullivan Award 20, 82, 131
Sutton, Mary 3
swimming 37–40, 40–43, 88–91, 138–
  142
Switzer, Katherine 66
Szewinska, Irena 150–152, 155

Tarzan's Revenge 43
Temple, Ed 147, 153
Tennis 3, 5, 6, 12, 22–25, 32–34,
  43–47, 78–81, 81–85, 91–94, 96–
  100, 101–104, 115–118
Tennis Hall of Fame 52, 81, 100
Thiel College 34
Thorpe, Jim 11
Thucydides 1
tickertape parade 39
Tickey, Bertha 112
Title IX 7
Topping, Dan 19
Totschnig, Brigitte 132
Tourisheva, Ludmila 76
track and field 5, 6, 11–12, 19–22, 54–
  58, 69–71, 85–89, 104–107, 145–
  148, 150–153, 156
trapshooting 48
Trevino, Lee 125
Tulsa University 126
Tuxedo Park 3
Tyus, Wyomia 152, 153–156

UCLA 20, 104–105
USO 71

Vanderbilt, Harold 54
Van Wie, Virginia 30
Vardon, Harry 60
Vare, Glenna see Collett, Glenna
Vare Trophy 31, 127, 160

Virginia Slims 118, 135
Vlasto, Julie 24
Von Saltza, Chris 13

Wagner, Mary 6
Waitz, Grete 68, 156–159
Walsh, Stella 56–58
Warner Brothers 42
Watson, Maud 32
Weissmuller, Johnny 74
Welsh, Priscilla 158, 159
Wembley Stadium 70, 76
Wentzel, Hanni 133, 143, 145
Wethered, Joyce 30, 58–60
Whitworth, Kathy 127, 159–162
Wightman, Helen Hotchkiss 52
Wightman Cup 24, 92
Wilhemus 70
Williams, Esther 71–72
Williams, Lucinda 147
Wills, Helen 6, 11, 22–25, 46, 78, 94, 100, 103, 115

Wimbledon 3, 6, 23–25, 32–34, 44–47, 78–81, 82–85, 93–94, 99–100, 101–103, 115–117, 135–137
Witt, Katerina, 5, 8, 16, 110, 162–165
Women's International Bowling Congress 2
Women's Swimming Association of New York 38
World Cup Skiing 132, 142–145
World Team Tennis 118
Worplesdon Tourney 60
Wright, Mickey 127, 160, 165–167

Yonkers, New York 4
Young, Sheila 168–171

Zaharias, Babe see Didrikson, Babe
Zaharias, George 11
Ziegfeld showgirls 42